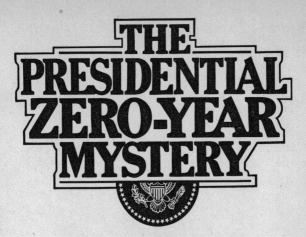

THE PRESIDENTIAL ZERO-YEAR MYSTERY

By Dr. David A. Lewis
and Darryl E. Hicks

D1399958

aven books
Division of Logos International
Plainfield, N.J. 07060

THE PRESIDENTIAL ZERO-YEAR MYSTERY
Copyright © 1980 by Logos International
Printed in the United States of America
Library of Congress Catalog Card Number: 80-84091
International Standard Book Number: 0-88270-490-7
Logos International
Plainfield, New Jersey 07060

Acknowledgments

Special thanks to Mona Lewis, Karen Hicks, Mike Florence and Mabel Hicks for research assistance, help in the preparation of the manuscript, and personal encouragement.

The authors wish to express gratitude also to various unnamed sources who provided key documents and previously unpublished information.

About the Authors

Dr. David A. Lewis is an expert on Middle Eastern affairs, co-author of *The Todd Phenomenon* (New Leaf Press), and author of an upcoming book on cults, as well as *The Daniel Factor*, a book on the future of Israel in light of Bible prophecy.

Darryl Hicks is head researcher and writer for a nationally syndicated television program. He has written numerous personality profiles featured in national magazines and is the author of several books, one dealing with religion among the superstars of Nashville, *God Comes to Nashville*.

Contents

1

The Death Cycle

Along with the sorrow, there is a desperate and howling note over the land. We must pray on our knees, but when we get up from them we cry with the poet: "Do not go gentle into that good night. Rage, rage, against the dying of the light." (Alistair Cooke [written two days after the assassination of President John F. Kennedy, the seventh consecutive zero-year president to die in office])

It was like a ghost haunting the convention. Everyone was thinking about it, but everybody was afraid to talk about it. (A leading publisher and historian speaking about the so-called "zero factor" in response to a talk show host's question about one of the 1980 political conventions)

The worst thing about history is that every time it repeats itself the price goes up. Of the many strange phenomena connected with the relatively young United States of America, one of the strangest and most incredible is *The Presidential Zero-Year Mystery*.

The basic facts are well-known: during the past 140 years, no United States president elected to that office on a year ending in zero has survived his term (or terms). Of the thirty-nine men who have held our nation's highest elected position, only eight have died while in office. And of those eight men, seven have been zero-year presidents.

William Henry Harrison was elected president on November 3, 1840. He died on April 4, 1841, just one month to the day after taking the oath of office. The cause was "bilious pleurisy" (probably pneumonia). On Inauguration Day, "Old Tippecanoe" stood bareheaded and without an overcoat. This unusual behavior, which resulted in his death, still baffles many historians.

Abraham Lincoln was elected to his first term on November 2, 1860 (and to his second term in 1864). After several reported assassination plots had been thwarted,

Lincoln was murdered on April 14, 1865, in a relatively unguarded theater box. The controversy surrounding John Wilkes Booth still shrouds the historic killing.

James A. Garfield became president-elect on November 2, 1880. On July 2, 1881, just months after his inauguration, a demented office seeker, Charles J. Guiteau, shot the president twice. On September 19 of that same year, Garfield died. Questionable medical practices and Guiteau's motives still remain historic mysteries.

William McKinley, a reportedly gentle, sincere man, sought to be president in 1888 and 1892. Finally in 1896, he reached his lifelong goal. Then in 1900, he won a reelection bid. On September 6, 1901, a young anarchist named Leon Czolgosz murdered the president. The president's secretary had tried to stop plans for the president to stand shaking hands in Buffalo, New York, but was overruled. McKinley died eight days after Czolgosz's ploy, and though the nation was gripped with sorrow and humiliation, the real reasons for medical inaccuracies and a supposed plot went unreported.

Warren G. Harding was elected on November 2, 1920. After three years of a scandal-filled term, the president was in Seattle, Washington, when he fell ill, allegedly of food poisoning. He proceeded to San Francisco, where doctors said he had pneumonia. Other sources also cited heart trouble, so the exact nature of his terminal illness is shrouded in mystery. His wife was accused in a poisoning plot, but the allegations remained only theoretical. Finally on August 2, 1923, Harding died, and the casebooks were closed. Or were they?

Franklin Delano Roosevelt, beloved and berated father of the New Deal, was elected to the Presidency for an unprecedented third term in 1940 as the nation mobilized for war. Then in 1945, one month after his fourth inauguration, the ailing president died in Warm Springs, Georgia. At first, he was mourned as the all-conquering hero, but within months, historians began sorting through reports of a sometimes splendid, sometimes sordid career. Supposed suicide reports also surfaced, especially after Mrs. Roosevelt refused to allow the casket to be opened. Even today, the mystery surrounding Roosevelt's death has continued to be the subject of spicy innuendo and historic debate.

John Fitzgerald Kennedy, on November 8, 1960, became the youngest man and the first Catholic ever elected to the Presidency. He was both the most popular and the most despised man elected to the nation's highest office during recent history. If he would have lived, perhaps historians could give more accurate descriptions of his professional career, but on November 22, 1963, his brilliant and bewildering term was permanently destroyed by a Dallas assassination, a murder that has since filled books, motion pictures, and conversations with suspense, mystery, and nonfitting puzzles.

While still a presidential candidate, Sen. John Kennedy made several interesting remarks while addressing the "coincidental" zero-year cycle:

> The historical curiosity is indeed thought-provoking: Since 1840 every man who has entered the White House in a year ending with a zero has not lived to leave the White House alive. I feel that the future will have to necessarily answer this for itself—both as to my aspirations and my fate should I have the privilege of occupying the White House.
>
> On face value, I daresay, should anyone take this phenomenon to heart—anyone, that is, who aspires to change his address

to 1600 Pennsylvania Avenue—that most probably the landlord would be left with a "For Rent" sign hanging on the gate-house door. (The original of this letter is found in the Library of Presidential Papers, New York)

The senator, though obviously puzzled by the phenomenon, did not take the death cycle to heart. He became president; the White House became Camelot. Then his "aspirations" and "fate" were lost forever as he became the seventh victim of *The Presidential Zero-Year Mystery.*

Only Thomas Jefferson, elected president in 1800, and James Monroe, elected to the nation's highest office in 1820, escaped this so-called "zero factor." Zachary Taylor was the only nonzero-year president who died in office.

Amazing coincidences? Unlikely. The computerized odds against John F. Kennedy dying while in office were 78.5 billion to one. But he was the 1960 zero-year president. The past seven zero-year tragedies now form eerie backdrops for the present. Again and again since 1840, the zero factor has spelled tragedy for American presidents. Will it again rip America apart with another smoldering chapter of tragedy and questions? All of these issues and questions form a veiled historical backdrop for our 1980 zero-year president and for this—*The Presidential Zero-Year Mystery.*

Thinking is good, but without memory it wastes time drawing new blueprints of old castles. Thinking and memory together will create rather than retrace. (Anonymous)

It is natural to man to indulge in the illusions of hope. We are apt to shut our eyes against a painful truth. . . . Is this the part of wise men, engaged in a great and arduous struggle for liberty? Are we disposed to be of the number of those who, having eyes, see not, and having ears, hear not, the things which so nearly concern their temporal salvation? For my part, whatever anguish of spirit it may cost, I am willing to know the whole truth; to know the worst and to provide for it. (Patrick Henry ["Liberty or Death" speech to the Virginia House of Burgesses, 1775])

We live in the present;
We dream of the future,
But we learn eternal truths from the past.
(Madame Chiang Kai-shek)

The Zero-Year Presidents

I have been haunted. I have become increasingly convinced that a curse of death hangs over my head as long as I am President, and I have been frightened.

It is a foolish thing, I know that. But it has become an obsession that I cannot shake. It grew from the roots of my boyhood in the mountains, where there were ghosts all around and all of us knew of someone who had been cursed and was suffering or was dead because of that curse.

The death of Presidents elected in years ending with zero has occurred seven times. It's a coincidence, a capricious bit of numerology. In cold moments of logic, I know this. But I have come to believe it is something more sinister, something deadly—and I cannot rid myself of the belief. (From the fiction best seller *The Zero Factor* by William Oscar Johnson)

2

William Henry Harrison—
So Many Questions

*Sir, I wish you to understand the true
principles of the government. I wish
them carried out. I ask nothing more.*
(The last words spoken by President
Harrison, 12:30 A.M., Sunday, April 4,
1841)

During 1840, the Whig Party took the
gamble of nominating a man who was considered fairly old to run for the Presidency,
sixty-eight-year-old William H. Harrison.
The Whigs won the election but lost the
gamble—Harrison lived only one month after his ballyhooed inauguration, and he became the first president ever to die in office.

But his story is an amazing collection of
riddles. His father, Benjamin Harrison,
was one of the founding fathers of the
nation, a member of the Continental Army,

and a signer of the Declaration of Independence. He also had the dubious honor of being remembered for writing a lewd letter to General Washington, hoping to amuse him (unfortunately the letter was seized by a British patrol, and a forged insertion in the letter was added to brand both the intended recipient and the author as men of low morals). The salacious letter he was reported to have written and the whispers about his intimate affairs (slave women and Philadelphia prostitutes) had no lasting, detrimental effect upon Benjamin Harrison's prestige; he was later elected governor of Virginia; his son, William Henry, and his grandson, Benjamin, both held the office of President of the United States.

William was born on February 9, 1773, the son of Benjamin and Elizabeth Bassett. Like the aristocrat he was, he studied classics and history at Hampden-Sidney College, then began a program of medical study at Richmond under Benjamin Rush.

Then, during 1791, Harrison shocked many by switching from an interest in medicine to a career in the military. Within a short period, he was commissioned as an ensign in the Regular Army's First Infantry, and he left for the Northwest (the Ohio River to the Great Lakes), where he spent most of his life.

Armed with a copy of Cicero's works and his officer's commission (quickly signed by Washington through Benjamin's efforts), William arrived at Fort Washington (where Cincinnati is now located) and began his career under the command of General (Mad Anthony) Wayne, a popular military leader during the Revolution. Despite persistent reports that he would be the proverbial "chip off the old block" lady-charmer, he won a distinctive reputation as a clean-living, daring Indian fighter, pioneer, and All-American hero.

During William's early years in the army, he met the woman who was to become the most positive influence in his life. It was one brisk spring day in 1795, while on business for General Wayne in Lexington, Kentucky, that young Harrison met Anna Symmes. Anna was visiting her sister Maria in Lexington. To Harrison, the quiet, educated, slender, nineteen-year-old lady was like a refreshing wind after the years of exposure to the hearty frontier women in the Ohio forests. She obviously was attracted to him for many reasons, not the least of which were his family background and reputation as an army hero.

Anna Tuthill Symmes, dark-eyed and sedate, had been born in Flatbrook, New Jersey, July 25, 1773, the daughter of Col. John Cleves Symmes. After an illustrious military career during the Revolution, Symmes became a member of the postwar Continental Congress, and in 1788, while a member of that Congress, he contracted for a million acres of land between the Great and Little Miami Rivers (in present-day Ohio) and also received a Northwest Territory judgeship.

Judge Symmes hardly approved of Harrison as a suitor for his oldest daughter; in fact, he said "no" when young Harrison asked for Anna's hand in marriage. It was 1795, and though William had seen successful campaigns in the army, he had little money. A thrifty army life seemed unthinkable. In addition, some scandalous tales concerning the lieutenant's conduct were going the rounds. Judge Symmes commanded Harrison, "Stay away from my daughter!" In reality, despite the stated disapproval of the elder Symmes, Anna and William were wed on November 25, 1795, in North Bend, Ohio (the soon-to-be-furious judge happened to be out of town on business).

"How do you expect to support my daughter?" the judge asked when he and the new bridegroom met two weeks after the ceremony. Historians report that Harrison fingered his scabbard and said, "My sword is my means of support, sir!" Supposedly the matter was settled peaceably when the Harrisons named their first son after the judge.

Despite the melodrama accompanying the marriage, Anna proved to be a tremendous faith-force in Harrison's life. She was a devout Presbyterian who influenced William to begin attending church regularly. Her life was to be filled with tragedies, sickness, and disgrace, but she remained deeply religious, always turning to her Bible and her church for solace and support. Even in her pain, she demonstrated a Christian concern for humanity. Sol Barzman, in the book *The First Ladies*, recounts these words that were spoken about Anna:

> Every public and private charity was near her heart, and received liberally from her hand. But those who enjoyed her bounty knew not of its source. To a poor minister she would write: "Accept this

trifle from a friend"; to the Bethel Sabbath school, "This is but a poor widow's mite"; to the suffering poor of the city, "Please distribute this from one who wishes it was a thousand times more."

But Anna is seldom remembered by historians except as "William's invalid wife who outlived him by a quarter-century." She, in fact, helped him gain the reputation (previously tarnished) as a completely honest, happily married man. She bore him ten children. Mostly, she seemed very concerned that her husband be involved in the great Protestant religious awakening during the early 1800s. Sadly, at least until his death, Harrison's faith proved dependent upon his "inherited" Episcopalian tradition and his wife's subtle admonitions.

As Anna's faith was born from the many tragedies she witnessed during her life, William's ego was built upon his many victories in the military and political arenas. After resigning from the army in 1798, he became secretary of the Northwest Territory, and he was its first delegate to Congress. He helped obtain legislation dividing the territory into the Northwest and Indiana Territories, and in 1801 he became governor of the Indiana Territory, serving twelve years. While he was governor, he led a force of nine hundred troops to victory at the Battle of Tippecanoe River during 1811 (hence the nickname, "Old Tippecanoe"). Already a national folk hero, he won more military laurels during the War of 1812 as brigadier general and commander of the army in the Northwest. At the Battle of the Thames (Michigan) on October 5, 1813, he defeated the combined British and Indian forces and killed the great Shawnee Chief, Tecumseh.

After the war with the British, Harrison resigned from the army, reportedly in a political ploy. In 1816 he was elected to Congress from Ohio. Later he served as a United States senator and minister to Colombia (1828). Though his immediate family had been tainted by disgrace, Harrison seemed likely to succeed as a professional politician. Tall, slim, and erect, he looked impressive in the saddle. He did not drink or gamble and refused to be drawn into suicidal duels, even though such practices were then considered extremely manly and causes for much boasting. To the Whig Party insiders, the western hero seemed a sure vote-getter. He seemed naive, manageable, and was chosen as the Whig's "patsy."

Harrison ran against Van Buren for the Presidency in 1836 and made a poor showing, but the "stamp of approval" given him by Thurlow Weed, the New York "boss" of the Whig Party, virtually insured not only the party's candidacy four years later, but the Presidency as well. Weed was the tall, dark manipulator who combined political victories with lucrative government contracts.

The election of 1840 marked an elaborate attempt to "develop" a made-to-order president through power and money that had been wielded unscrupulously. It was the first elaborate national campaign built around everything but the issues: on Harrison's military exploits against the Indians, especially at Tippecanoe; on his service as a civil and military leader in "the West." Campaign posters pictured Harrison as "The Hero of Tippecanoe" or as "The Farmer of North Bend." "Honest John" Tyler, another Weed vassal, was "chosen" as Harrison's running mate—hence "Tippecanoe and Tyler too," which became the theatrical Whig slogan at the largest frenzied political rallies and mass meetings ever held in America's history.

One of the more ironic twists during the Harrison-Van Buren campaigns came through a media jeer. A writer who was sympathetic toward the Democrats comically suggested a way to get Harrison to relinquish his nomination: "Upon condition of his receiving a pension of two thousand dollars, a barrel of cider, General Harrison would no doubt consent to withdraw his pretentions and spend his days in a log cabin on the banks of the Ohio."

Rather than responding to the obvious Weed "buying power," the Whigs turned the Baltimore newsman's statement into political "gold," adopting the log cabin and hard cider as their emblems, to show that their man was a plain country boy, in contrast to the fancy, wine-drinking Van Buren. In spite of the facts that Harrison had not been born in a cabin, that he did not live in one (his North Bend house had twenty-two rooms), and that his aristocratic tastes did not include hard cider, fiction won over fact. The "log cabin campaign" was a national frolic. In jubilant parades throughout the country, people carried log cabins and casks of hard cider (props first provided by Thurlow Weed in New York rallies, then picked up by the

E.C. Booz Company of Philadelphia—the word "booze" came from the log-cabin-shaped glass kegs).

From one city to the next, the pattern was identical: as the crowds became more intoxicated on the supplied "booze," the official song leader, Joseph Hoaxie, would lead the riotous throngs in the increasingly popular song:

> For Tippecanoe and Tyler, too—
> Tippecanoe and Tyler, too;
> And with them we'll beat little Van, Van,
> Van is a used-up man;
> And with them we'll beat little Van.

After the pro-Whig tunes, Harrison or one of Weed's cohorts would attack the Democrats. The Democratic rule for four years was distasteful to many because of the 1837 depression and the reported elegant habits of Van Buren. So effective was the Whig tool of attacking the Democrats as a party, rather than attacking the issues, that the tide of an expected victory soon mended the broken ranks of the Whig Party. Even Daniel Webster, a Whig who considered Harrison an "idiot," began campaigning for the party's candidate, not so much from conviction as from a desire to control him afterward.

As for Harrison, the campaign was an endless affair of manipulation by Weed and the "inner circle." For the most part, Harrison was not even allowed to campaign for himself until late in the running, and then he was only permitted to read carefully prepared messages.

Insiders knew Harrison realized he was Weed's pawn, but seemed to have little control over the political moves. Albert Steinberg, in the book *The First Ten*, recounts a letter written by Nicholas Biddle, Harrison's national campaign manager, to a local manager:

> Let him (Harrison) say not a single word about his principles, or his creed—let him say nothing, promise nothing. Let no committee, no convention—no town meeting ever extract from him a single word about what he thinks now, or what he will do hereafter. Let the use of pen and ink be wholly forbidden as if he were a mad poet in Bedlam.

Weed formed a "Conscience-Keeping Committee" to voice Harrison's "thoughts" to the public. Ghostwriters answered political questions. By the summer of 1840, Harrison began to make campaign appearances, partially to dispel rumors that he was in ill health. By then his writing crew had prepared a seven-point statement on Harrison's ideas on the Presidency. Actually, it was not altogether necessary that Harrison talk much at all; the "booze" parties and songfests occupied most of the public's attention. Harrison's main function (at the rallies he did attend) was to walk around briskly (showing that he was in good health). He was never allowed to wander far from a member of the "Conscience-Keeping Committee."

As the campaign neared its climax, the Democrats and Van Buren believed that only the most unsuspecting voter would cast a ballot for Harrison. In effect, Van Buren's stand on issues was overshadowed by Harrison's image as the "true American frontiersman" and the "common man's man" (and the countless barrels of hard cider and cigars provided by Thurlow Weed certainly helped as well). The popular vote was close, but the electoral vote was one-sided: 234 for Harrison; only sixty for President Van Buren. A western newspaper summed up the irony of the election best when it exclaimed, "Van Buren had been sung down, lied down, and drank down!"

Later voting fraud allegations were proven, connecting Weed's crooked poll practices from state to state. In addition, it was reported that Thurlow Weed had made considerable commitments to British agents promising business and political influence if Harrison was elected to office.

Regardless of the methods, William Henry Harrison was elected to the nation's highest office on November 3, 1840. The news was received back in North Bend with mixed emotions. In the book *Old Tippecanoe*, Freeman Cleaves quotes Mrs. Harrison as having said:

> I wish that my husband's friends had left him where he is, happy and contented in retirement.

Anna continued to show little enthusiasm for her husband's "victory" and stayed behind in Ohio (citing ill health) when Harrison left for Washington on January 26, 1841. The president arrived in the nation's capital on his sixty-eighth birthday, Tuesday, February 9, and he was promptly heralded as a bad omen. He was blamed openly by the Democrats for the heavy snowstorm that blanketed Washington the day he arrived. Also, curiously, the president-elect was connected to the fact that the Senate scroll with *E Pluribus Unum* on it had fallen off the wall upon his arrival. Another claim was that a rope made of flags from all the states and strung across Pennsylvania Avenue had strangely broken as Harrison approached. Undoubtedly the reports of ill omen partly resulted from "sour grapes," but truth *is* sometimes stranger than fiction.

Inauguration Day, March 4, 1841, dawned brisk and blustery. A dozen bands played during the assembling of military corpsmen. Rejecting the fine coach offered by Baltimore Whigs, Harrison rode Old Whitey, his trusted mount, down Pennsylvania Avenue in the grand procession that extended nearly two miles. For some unknown and unexplainable reason, the president-elect wore no overcoat, and his hat was in his hand as he bowed and waved to the crowd.

At the noon hour, the presidential assemblage moved to a platform outdoors from the Senate chamber. 50,000 people roared a greeting, then silence fell as Harrison addressed the nation.

A cold, northeast wind chilled even the

spectators in heavy winter apparel, yet—
oddly enough—once again Harrison stood
bareheaded and without gloves or an overcoat for one hour and forty minutes as
he puppeted the Webster-written, Henry
Clay-edited inaugural address. Why he
chose to brave the wintry cold during the
parade and address perhaps no one will
ever know. Perhaps he had no choice—
especially since his political strategists
were intent on dispelling rumors that Harrison was in ill health.

Regardless, by the time he finished his
8500-word speech (ironically, it was the
longest inaugural address in history, and
it was given by the man who spent the
least amount of time in office), Harrison's
lips were blue. Though he was thoroughly
chilled, for the third time during the day
he was escorted, without wraps, through a
long, slow-moving procession to the executive mansion.

Unsurprisingly, Harrison came down
with a heavy chest cold the next day. A
troublesome cough persisted. He did not
feel well, yet began receiving a never-end-
ing line of office seekers and well-wishers.

A constant lack of judgment despite his
worsening condition finally took its dread-

ful toll. On one occasion, while out for a walk, Harrison was caught in a downpour and returned soaking wet to the White House, but instead of spending the rest of the day indoors, he walked through the slush to a nearby house to offer a friend a diplomatic post. Shortly thereafter, he was sitting in a cabinet meeting and was suddenly stricken by a shaking chill that continued for fifteen minutes. On March 27, he sent for a physician. Four doctors eventually attended him, drawing blood with suction cups, then covering the wounds with stinging ointments to kill the escaping germs ("bleeding" to get the germs out was still a common practice). He was given harsh purgatives: rhubarb, castor oil, and calomel. Still the fever increased with symptoms of pneumonia and intestinal inflammation. The disease was announced as "bilious pleurisy." He was administered opium and brandy, presumably so he could stand the torture. Back home in North Bend, his wife was reluctantly getting ready to go to Washington.

Washington was buzzing with gossip concerning the fate of spoils seekers should the president die. As it turned out, it was every man for himself.

One month to the day after taking the oath of office, William Henry Harrison uttered his last words to Doctor Worthington:

Sir, I wish you to understand the true principles of the government. I wish them carried out. I ask nothing more.

Death came soon after at 12:30 A.M., Sunday, April 4. Anna Symmes Harrison got the news just as she was about to depart for Washington.

Andrew Jackson remarked sadly, "A kind and overruling Providence has interfered to prolong our glorious Union. For surely, Tyler (Harrison's successor) will stay the corruption of this clique who has got into power by deluding the people by the grossest of slanders" (As quoted in Steinberg's *The First Ten*). In retrospect, William Henry Harrison's short-lived presidential career has been viewed by most historical writers as contemptuously as he was viewed by his peers. By both he was labeled a political pawn, a dubious prestige that alludes to cynicism and scorn.

Hope has been spoken for Harrison in a spiritual vein. As a churchgoer in Washington, he occupied pew 45 in St. John's Episcopal Church. Soon after his arrival in Washington, he visited the city's only bookstore and complained loudly to the proprietor that he had not been able to find a Bible in the White House. The historian Steinberg quotes the newly elected president as insisting, "The Bible ought to be a part of the furniture of the house."

During his fatal illness, Harrison requested that someone read Psalm 103, and he seemed "overpowered with emotion" as the passage was read:

> Bless the Lord, O my soul: and all that is within me, bless his holy name.
> Bless the Lord, O my soul, and forget not all his benefits:
> Who forgiveth all thine iniquities; who healeth all thy diseases;
> Who redeemeth thy life from destruction; who crowneth thee with lovingkindness and tender mercies; . . .
>
> The Lord is merciful and gracious, slow to anger, and plenteous in mercy.
> He will not always chide: neither will he keep his anger for ever.
> He hath not dealt with us after our sins; nor rewarded us according to our iniquities.
> For as the heaven is high above the earth, so great is his mercy toward them that fear him.

As far as the east is from the west, so far hath he removed our transgressions from us. . . .

Bless the Lord, all his works in all places of his dominion: bless the Lord, O my soul.

After this emotional moment, he openly thanked the Lord for His goodness. Then came the relapse and his eventual death. In spiritual terms, who knows whether the president found eternal peace so close to the end of his life? His wife certainly had been a faithful influence, even through the scandalous campaign. Perhaps the emotions he exhibited were guilt-filled relapses as he faced death. Maybe they were the final struggles for spiritual freedom—freedom from human bondage to a giant political machine in which he was trapped.

Regardless, on Wednesday, April 7, a heavy cannon boomed, audible throughout Washington, signaling the final day of mourning. At 11:30 A.M., Rev. Hawley, the rector of St. John's, recalled the president's church-attendance habits and the Bible he had purchased recently, and intoned the reading from the Psalms and First Corinthians, "I am the resurrection and the life."

Shortly thereafter, his body was laid to

rest in Hamilton County, Ohio. So many questions were unanswered—even during the tempestuous, irregular term John Tyler filled.

Was Harrison's death a grim reminder to America that God would not allow the nation, purposely founded upon His precepts, to wallow in political corruption?

Was the term of the ninth president, as some astrologers and occultists claim, cut short because of the zodiac-conjunction of Jupiter and Saturn, and if so, would that same tragedy occur every twenty years under the Jupiter/Saturn conjunction?

Was the president's death closely linked to some type of worldwide or supernatural conspiracy?

Is the death cycle an amazing coincidence or an eerie curse? The only answer historians can offer is one inexplicable fact: from 1840 until now, each American president elected in the zero year has not survived his term of office. William Henry Harrison (1773-1841) was only the beginning of *The Presidential Zero-Year Mystery.*

3

Abraham Lincoln—
A Shrouded Plot

If you are as happy, my dear sir, on entering this house as I am in leaving it and returning home, you are the happiest man in this country. (Ex-president Buchanan to President Lincoln on Inauguration Day, March 4, 1861)

Dust filtered through the streets that cold March morning as Lincoln rode to the Capitol in a carriage with the retiring president, James Buchanan. Buchanan had served his country well, but the growing emotions connected to the slavery issue and the panic of 1857 had been incredible burdens. The white-haired bachelor from Pennsylvania seemed relieved to turn over the helm of the nation to the tall, gaunt man in ill-fitting clothes from Illinois. Buchanan had reportedly been threatened with assassination by both proslavery and antislavery extremists.

There were soldiers beside the presidential carriage and sharpshooters on Pennsylvania Avenue rooftops—all prepared to fire if an assassination attempt was made. It was common knowledge that some men had sworn that "Honest Abe" would die before taking the oath of office.

Still, Lincoln rode slowly up the broad avenue, seemingly oblivious to the threats, smiling, compassionate, his rawboned hands actively waving to the crowd. Many people lined the streets to catch a glimpse of this man, since little was known about him. In reality, his meteoric rise from obscurity and failure was a mystery to casual observers and political analysts alike.

He was so unknown, in fact, that the country as a whole first heard the story of Lincoln's life just five months before his nomination, when the Republican hopeful, at a friend's request, had written a letter that briefly outlined his erstwhile career (an article based on the following edited letter was widely printed throughout the country):

I was born February 12, 1809, in Hardin County, Kentucky. My parents were both born in Virginia, of undistinguished families—second families, perhaps I should say. My mother, who died in my tenth year, was of a family of the name of Hanks.

My paternal grandfather, Abraham Lincoln, emigrated from Rockingham County, Virginia, to Kentucky about 1781 or 1782 . . . where he was killed by Indians. . . .

My father, at the death of his father, was but six years of age, and he grew up literally without education. He removed from Kentucky to . . . Indiana in my tenth year. . . . It was a wild region, with many bears and other wild animals still in the woods. There I grew up. There were some schools, so called, but no qualification was ever required of a teacher beyond "readin', writin', and cipherin' " to the rule of three. . . . There was absolutely nothing to excite ambition for education. Of course, when I came of age I did not know much. Still, somehow, I could read, write, and cipher . . . but that was all. I have not been to school since.

After summarizing his life and career—general farm work until he was twenty-two years old; store clerk in New Salem, Illinois; captain during the Black Hawk War; eight years as a member of the Illinois legislature (1834-42), during which he studied law (admitted to the bar in 1836); a lawyer in Springfield, Illinois, after a move there in 1837; a member of Congress (1847-49)—and without mentioning his marriage to Mary Todd (1842), his children, or his defeat for the United States Senate (1858)—Lincoln closed his letter with the following words:

> If any personal description of me is thought desirable, it may be said that I am, in height, six feet four inches, nearly; lean in flesh, weighing on an average of one hundred and eighty pounds; dark complexion, with coarse black hair and grey eyes. No other marks or brands recollected.

Despite his obvious modesty, Lincoln was to be one of the landmarks of American history. His preparation for this bittersweet moment in time had been one marked by tragedy, self-education, and introspection.

His natural mother, Nancy Hanks Lincoln, certainly did not know the prominence she would have in history. Schooled in Virginia, she was a woman who was intellectual, devoted, and faithful. On Sundays she would read to her children from the Bible and pray with them. During those formative years, she impressed her ideals, convictions, and drive upon her son. Even after he made the incredible rise from a log cabin to the White House, Abraham Lincoln would speak of his mother: "I remember her prayers, and they have always followed me. They have clung to me all my life."

Lincoln's mother died of "milk sickness" in the fall of 1818, but her convictions and love of knowledge were passed to Abe. His cousin, Dennis Hanks, was once quoted as saying, "I [have] never seen Abe after he was twelve that he didn't have a book somewheres around." Especially after Tom Lincoln took a new wife, Sarah Bush Johnson, a kind and gentle widow who brought her three children to the Lincoln cabin, Abraham was encouraged to read whatever he could lay his hands upon, reading and rereading the books until he understood them—by sunlight, by candlelight, by firelight—whenever he had a spare moment. He had access to only a few books, but they were the best—the Lincolns owned a Bible, and he was able to borrow such favorites as *Aesop's Fables*, *Pilgrim's Progress*, and *The Life of George Washington*.

Sarah Lincoln was especially fond of her stepchildren. She encouraged her lanky stepson to speak freely of his dreams and to continue learning. When Lincoln became a man and was in the nation's limelight, he spoke of his stepmother in special terms:

God bless my mother; all that I am or ever hope to be, I owe to her.

So it was an unusual man with a mostly unknown past who sat in the carriage with President Buchanan. In all history there would never be a more dramatic example of the times calling forth a "man of the hour." He had risen above every conceivable obstacle: humble birth, ignorance and poverty in the frontier wilderness; a relatively unsuccessful career without advantages or known connections; too human to be a professional politician (or the favorite of the professionals); too philosophical and too humorous ever to be a great historical figure. Yet against all the odds, though he was the second choice of many Americans, though he received only 40 percent of the votes during the 1860 Presidential Election (it was a four-way race), yet he received 180 votes in the electoral college and was duly certified as the President of the

United States.

When he left Springfield on February 11, 1861, for the trek to Washington, he was known as a man who had learned how to make bargains and trade for advantages, as a man who had married a beautiful and wealthy woman (Mary Todd) who loved him, scolded him, and gave him three sons.

Yet, even as he embarked for Washington, there was much that few people knew. Skepticism about Lincoln's character had drifted through his presidential campaign. As his associates and friends struggled to promote the Republican nominee as "Honest Abe," there were missing puzzle pieces. Carl Sandburg's sensitive biography about Lincoln spoke quizzically about the impressions of "Honest Abe":

> There was about him something spreading and elusive and mysterious . . . something out-of-the-ordinary . . . in Springfield and elsewhere, whispers floated of circumstances so misty and strange that political friends wished they could be cleared up and made respectable.

A century later, a popular author came across clues and lithographs signed by Lincoln that seemed to conclusively point to evidence that Lincoln was the father of an illegitimate girl born in Hazelwood, Illinois, in either 1855 or 1856. A montage of strange associations and related episodes in his life while in Springfield were uncovered. His love for Ann Rutledge was common knowledge even during the 1800s, but certainly there was something more unsavory than a "lost love" connected to Lincoln's prolonged absences from home—of which his wife frequently complained. Yet these mysteries remained hidden for a century—fortunately. If his political opposition in 1860 could have learned the reason behind the whispers, or that he had had a daughter out of wedlock, he would never have been the zero-year president. He might never been treated as one of the most important men in history, and ironically, might never have been forced to face the incredible struggles that loomed ahead, nor the fateful tragedy that would shake and enshroud the nation.

In fact, why he was chosen to be president in 1860, when so many illustrious, well-known men like William H. Seward, Henry Clay, and Stephen A. Douglas (Lincoln's longtime antagonist) had not been picked, nobody can truthfully say.

But that day in March, as the newly elected president addressed the throngs gathered in Washington, he was not the man of mystery or melancholy, nor was he the unsuccessful man who had once contemplated suicide—he was a man of strength, honesty, and deep humanity. The man who would become a legend as the Great Emancipator spoke passionately to his increasingly separated nation:

> There needs to be no bloodshed or violence, and there shall be none unless it be forced upon the national authority.
> Intelligence, patriotism, Christianity, and a firm reliance upon Him who has never yet forsaken this favored land are still competent to adjust in the best way all our present difficulty.

War clouds hung heavily over the president as he spoke; it was no mistake that Lincoln was the first president whose military escort was really a guard instead of an honorary escort. There had been, and would continue to be, numerous threats and plots against this most loved and most hated man.

Those war clouds exploded when the Confederate batteries began to bombard Fort Sumter, South Carolina. At 4:30 A.M., on April 12, 1861, the first cannon boomed, and the bloodiest war ever fought on the North American continent began.

During the next five years, as thousands of American boys died in furious battles across the torn land, Lincoln and his household were also plunged into a spiritual realm, an unseen struggle that sometimes only the closest observers were able to see.

Lincoln was a confessing believer in Jesus Christ. Even his enemies admitted this. He realized the importance of spiritual strength, and on August 12, only months after taking office, he proclaimed a national fast day:

> Whereas it is fit and becoming in all people, at all times, to acknowledge and revere the supreme government of God; to bow in humble submission to His chastisements; to confess and deplore their sins and transgressions, in the full conviction that the fear of the Lord is the beginning of wisdom; and to pray with all fervency and contrition for the pardon of their past offenses, and for a blessing upon their present and prospective action:
>
> And whereas when our own beloved country, once, by the blessing of God, united, prosperous, and happy, is now afflicted with faction and civil war, it is peculiarly

fit for us to recognize the hand of God in this terrible visitation, and in sorrowful remembrance of our own faults and crimes as a nation and as individuals, to humble ourselves before Him and to pray for His mercy—to pray that we may be spared further punishment though most justly deserved; that our arms may be blessed and made effectual for the establishment of law, order, and peace throughout the wide extent of our country.

Therefore, I Abraham Lincoln, President of the United States, do appoint the last Thursday of September next as a day of humiliation, prayer, and fasting for all the people of the nation.

The closeness of the spiritual battle struck within the household when Willie, the Lincoln's preteen son, died from typhoid fever. The mournful father could not eat, could not concentrate on the growing national problems, could not talk with his friends. He wandered through the White House, weeping and restless. Mrs. Lincoln, aware of his inner turmoil, asked help from the Reverend Francis Vinton, who in turn spoke with the president, shocking him out of his woe-stricken condition by accusing him of self-indulgence. The pastor then quoted comforting words from the

Gospel of Matthew, "God is not the God of the dead, but of the living" (Matt. 22:32). Tears silently flowing down the president's deeply lined face reflected the coming calm. "Alive?" he mused. Dr. Vinton nodded, adding that Willie was alive in paradise. Lincoln was a renewed man as he resumed his duties.

Unfortunately, Mrs. Lincoln—though she knew that a fierce spiritual battle surrounded the family—became the "weak link." She had no doubt been aware that her gentle husband had loved another, perhaps more than her, and she allowed these feelings to surface on occasion. At any other time in history, Mary Todd Lincoln might have been a popular first lady. She had been born to wealth in Kentucky, was politically astute and was attractive, and as Abraham began his unpredictable climb in politics, she dreamed of the day when her Abe would win the highest office. Just as she appeared to be tenderhearted, deeply religious, and an affectionate wife and mother, she was also driven by an excessive ambition. At times her temper, jealousy, and extravagance became uncontrollable.

Once inside the White House (and she

was more responsible for this than most people will ever know), everything seemed to work against her. The time was catastrophic, a period in which her extravagant tastes were out of place. Even when she was overwhelmed with grief over Willie's death, she got little sympathy. With a husband too busy and preoccupied with national conflicts, and with a burning resentment toward other Washington women to whom—at the most—the president was merely courteous, the first lady became a brittle, bitter woman.

At one time, Lincoln feared that his wife's outbursts of temper, severe headaches, and strange acts might best be cured in a mental institution (she was hospitalized eventually after the tragedy in 1865). Grieving over Willie's death, Mary—once deeply religious—began to lose her spiritual struggle. She reportedly held spiritist seances in the executive mansion's red room, trying to communicate with her dead son. These actions most certainly embarrassed her worried husband, especially since the occult realm posed an unwelcome threat to the heretofore Christian household.

Then Mrs. Lincoln's reckless spending was another source of trouble. Those close to the family have alleged that her debts for clothing alone ran over $25,000. Her habits were bizarre—one item on her list was for three hundred pairs of gloves.

Lincoln's method of handling her generally included attempts to make her chuckle; each time, he softly addressed her as "Mother" and tried to soothe her. Often—to escape the constant glare of the wary public—he would guide her to private quarters.

This ensuing struggle continued through Lincoln's first term. By 1864 many Republican politicians thought the country had had enough of Lincoln. One was Thurlow Weed, a cunning guidemaster of public opinion (he had served in this role for William Henry Harrison). "Boss" Weed said "the people are wild for peace" and that it would be impossible for Lincoln to be reelected. Horace Greeley, editor of the New York *Tribune*, echoed Weed's feelings: "Mr. Lincoln is already beaten. He cannot be elected. We must have another ticket to save us from utter overthrow."

The majority of Republicans, however, had grown tired of Weed's maneuvering and had nominated Lincoln on the first ticket. To have done otherwise would have been an admission that the war policy of the Republican administration was incorrect.

"Don't swap horses" became the Grand Old Party's Unionist rally cry. Once again Lincoln won the election, polling 212 electoral votes to Democrat Gen. George B. McClellan's 21 votes. That reelection victory was a signal of the coming victorious end to the Civil War.

When the news finally came on April 9, 1865, of the capitulation by General Lee and the southern forces, all the cabinet—at the request of the president—dropped to their knees and offered thanksgiving to God. Tears and hushed silence filled the cabinet room.

Soon after, on April 11, 1865, the president called for a time of national thanksgiving, but from that time forward, observers noted his growing premonitions of a coming dreadful event. He had carried in his heart a feeling that he would die a violent death, a feeling that had admittedly been with him even before he had left Springfield to enter the White House after the 1860 election.

Now that the end of the war was a reality, Lincoln informed close friends of troublesome, recurring dreams. He spoke of dreams where he was carried on a dark ship to a distant shore, toward an unknown, unseen harbor.

One specific dream was so disturbing that he had described it in detail (quoted from Frank K. Kelly's *The Martyred Presidents*):

> There seemed to be a deathlike stillness about me. Then I heard subdued sobs, as if a number of people were weeping. I thought I left my bed and wandered downstairs.
>
> I arrived at the East Room, which I entered. There I met the sickening surprise. Before me was a catafalque, on which rested a corpse wrapped in funeral vestments. Around it were stationed soldiers who were acting as guards; and there was a throng of people, gazing mournfully upon the corpse, whose face was covered. "Who is dead in the White House?" I demanded of one of the soldiers. "The president," was his answer. "He was killed by an assassin." Then came a loud burst of grief from the crowd, which awoke me from my dream.

Lincoln tried to shrug off his wife's alarm when he described the dream, retorting that he couldn't let his life be controlled by mere nightmares. To another friend,

Ward Hill Lamon, the president talked about the dream but verbally tried to rationalize that the dream was not meant for himself.

It was. Throughout the war, Lincoln often attended the theater or the opera, mainly to take his mind off family and national problems. So it was on April 14.

The president's carriage left the White House about 8:15 P.M. and arrived at the theater somewhere around 8:30. Curtain time had been at 7:45, but the performance of Tom Taylor's comedy, *Our American Cousin*, was momentarily interrupted by the entrance of the president and his party (Mrs. Lincoln, Miss Clara Harris, and Miss Harris's fiancé, Major Henry Rathbone) replete with the orchestra blaring "Hail to the Chief."

After the party had entered boxes 7 and 8, the doors to both were closed but not locked. An usher took a seat in the vestibule where he could guard the entrance. John F. Parker of the Washington Police Department, who had been assigned as Lincoln's bodyguard, was also supposed to keep an eye on the presidential box that night, but he was apparently next door at a tavern (his dubious record with the force would make it seem quite unlikely that he would have been selected at all for such an august duty).

At 10:13, a pistol shot rang out. The president slumped in his seat. Major Rathbone sprang from his seat, but Booth unsheathed a seven-inch hunting knife, lunged at Rathbone (slashing a severe gash on the soldier's left arm), then jumped over the railing to the stage eleven feet below, breaking his left leg, yet brandishing his dagger as he limped across the stage, crazed, yelling something that sounded like *sic temper tyrannis* ("ever thus to tyrants"), and disappeared into the wings (to a waiting horse held by handyman Joseph "Peanuts" Burroughs). Three days later he was found in a barn near Port Royal, Virginia, and shot to death by a soldier (Boston Corbett) who fired without orders.

The wounded Lincoln was carried across the street into the nearest house, rented by an army private (William T. Clark). Army surgeon Charles Augustus Leale (who also had been at the play) and acting assistant surgeon Charles S. Taft began assessing the damage. There are conflicting reports— each surgeon pointing to the other as primarily responsible for the case. Eventually other doctors would examine the wound—Joseph Barnes, Robert Stone, Edward Curtis, and J.J. Woodward (who performed the autopsy). Additional doctors produced more conflicting stories.

The bullet had torn through his brain and rested behind one of his eyes (his *left* eye, according to Woodward; his *right* eye, according to Taft). Leale and Taft even disagreed on which pupil was dilated (a dilated pupil may indicate which side of the brain is damaged).

One major finding was clear to all the doctors—there was no hope. Despite attempts at cardiac massage and mouth-to-mouth resuscitation, at 7:22 the next morning, the heart of the lanky giant ceased.

Shortly before, as the sun began rising over Washington, it had begun to rain. It was certainly one of the most tragic days in the history of our nation. Secretary of War Edwin Stanton, as the president passed away, is said to have sadly summarized the scene for all historians—"Now he belongs to the ages."

As rain continued to fall upon the city, the word of Lincoln's death paralyzed the people. Newly freed slaves and soldiers who had fought for their freedom knelt outside the house to pray for their beloved president, but it was too late.

Mrs. Lincoln, in shock, began screaming, "Oh, that dreadful house! That dreadful house!" (Historians have been somewhat confused as to whether the reference was being made to the Clark house or the White House that she had both loved and hated.)

A black-draped funeral railway car bore Lincoln's body on the last journey from Washington to Springfield. The 1,700 miles took from April 21 to May 3. Thousands watched sadly as their fallen leader passed from town to hamlet to city. The sweetness of the Union victory and the promise of the coming peace had been turned to bitterness and sorrow. The war that nobody wanted was over, and there was no one to celebrate.

The mystery of his life, the strange journey from a cabin in Kentucky to the courtrooms of Illinois to the halls of Congress and then to the White House—all gave way to the ultimate mysteries surrounding his death.

Lincoln's remains were placed in the Oak Ridge Cemetery in Springfield. Buried with him there are his three sons, Eddie, Willie, and his beloved Tab. His firstborn son, Robert, lived until 1926. His wife, Mary Todd Lincoln (also buried in Oak Ridge), a loyal and devoted wife through the lean years of her husband's career, was a failure in the White House to which her early ambitions had pointed.

Two years after she left Washington, she put her finery on public sale; the country was astounded at the queer collection: a bolt of lace valued at four thousand dollars, a shawl worth two thousand, etc. In 1875, after a spiritual and physical nightmare, she was adjudged insane. She died in 1882, at the age of sixty-four.

There are still many questions. What were the underlying reasons for Abraham Lincoln rising from unsuccessful obscurity to the highest office in the land? Was it mere destiny? Or more?

What caused the incredible spiritual struggle during the five years in office?

That there had been plots to kill the president is common knowledge, but what made the plot of the madman Booth work? His cohorts were certainly not master-minds who could make all the pieces fit, or were they?

Why was the lock on the door to Lincoln's box broken just days before (and not repaired—even though it was known that the president often went to the theater)?

Why was such little attention given to posting guards outside the president's box, especially in light of other threats on his life?

Why was an ineffectual policeman like John F. Parker given the duty that night? Both Parker and John Wilkes Booth spent time during the play at Peter Taltavull's saloon next door. Was that mere coincidence?

Only one man could have given any insight into the dark picture—John Wilkes Booth. Why then—when Booth was trapped in a burning tobacco barn and surrounded by Union calvarymen—did Boston Corbett impulsively fire the fatal shot, despite orders not to shoot? Was it the act of a young patriot who was burning with revenge; was it a collusion between the police, the army, and Booth; or was it just another in the long list of unexplainable, bizarre circumstances? Or did Booth (as some historians say) commit suicide?

Certainly Booth must have realized the futility of his historic deed, but he remained firm in the conviction that he had done the right thing. He saw himself as the savior of the South. He had also fulfilled a childhood prophecy that he made to his friends that someday he would do something that would make his name "descend to posterity and never be forgotten." Just before his death, the moody actor murmured, "Tell Mother I died for my country. I have done what I thought was for the best." In so doing, John Wilkes Booth became infamous as the first man in history to kill a president of the United States.

If there was some conspiratorial plot—bigger than Booth—set on weakening national security and single-mindedness, the dastardly plot worked. The nation was thrown into a period of chaos much worse than the turmoil that occurred after Harrison's death. Lincoln's successor, Andrew Johnson, proved less effectual even than Harrison's vice-president (Tyler). Even Southerners felt Booth (and the others connected with the assassination) had done the nation a horrible disservice.

Perhaps, to paraphrase War Secretary Stanton's eulogy, the answers belong to the ages. After more than a century Stanton's words still ring true. So many questions remain about which even the best historians can only speculate. The unknown answers are all part of the legendary story of *The Presidential Zero-Year Mystery*.

4

James Abram Garfield— Medicine or Mystery?

My God! What is there in this place that a man should ever want to get into it? (President Garfield, speaking about the White House)

No, my work is done. (One of the last phrases spoken by President James Garfield at Francklyn Cottage by-the-Sea, Elberon, New Jersey)

Glory, glory, glory. (The last words of Charles J. Guiteau, Garfield's assassin, spoken just before the trapdoor opened, June 30, 1882)

As the twentieth president of the United States, he appeared to be much like a villain in a cloak-and-dagger play. On the surface he was somberly dressed, a scowling, bewhiskered figure.

In reality, he was probably one of the most Christian, scholarly (he used to entertain his friends by simultaneously writing Latin with one hand and Greek with the other), genial, easygoing, and warmhearted men ever to occupy the nation's highest office. Six feet tall, muscular, broad-shouldered, smooth in speech and swift in stride, his rags-to-riches career was legendary, even among the Horatio Alger stories that flourished during the Victorian Era.

But we can only imagine what this extraordinary man might have done as president. Certainly his motives seemed clear—antipoverty, antigreed and anticorruption. But mankind will never know how successful he might have been. An ex-evangelist, Charles Guiteau, ended the dream.

James Abram Garfield was born in a crude, one-room cabin on his father's frontier farm in Orange township, Ohio, on November 19, 1831. Abram, James's father, died from smoke inhalation before James reached two years of age, leaving Eliza Ballou and the five little Garfields practically destitute. The success of the family, and most notably, the success of James was a tribute to Eliza's quiet determination and faith in God. She often quoted favorite verses from the Bible, instilling a reservoir of faith that her children would someday live by:

> For I have learned, in whatsoever state I am, therewith to be content.
>
> I know both how to be abased, and I know how to abound: every where and in all things I am instructed both to be full and to be hungry, both to abound and to suffer need.
>
> I can do all things through Christ which strengtheneth me. (Phil. 4:11-13)

From the time he was three years old, young James developed a great love for reading and education. Besides helping his widowed mother, he also succeeded in earning enough—as a canal boat driver (he testified years later that God had saved him from drowning fourteen times), a carpenter, and a teacher (which included thrashing the local bully who had driven away the previous schoolteacher, after which Garfield promptly remarked, "Before learning comes understanding!")—to put himself through Geauga Seminary (Chester, Ohio), Hiram Eclectic Institute (a Disciples of Christ college in Ohio), and Williams College (Williamstown, Massachusetts).

Returning from Williams with honors in 1856, Garfield was made president of Hiram College, where he also devoted much time to evangelism and preaching. He was married on November 11, 1858, to his childhood sweetheart, Lucretia Rudolf; their family of seven children would include two sons who would hold prominent positions under Theodore Roosevelt and Woodrow Wilson.

The same drive that brought Garfield into the scholarly ranks carried him into public life. At twenty-seven, he was elected to the Ohio legislature. He found time to study law and was admitted to the bar just before the outbreak of the Civil War.

The gunfire at Fort Sumter changed the life of James Garfield, just as that bombardment altered the lives of every man in his generation. On the day Fort Sumter fell, he hurried to Ohio Governor William Dennison and asked for a commission in the Ohio infantry. Convinced that slavery had to be destroyed, he had once said:

> I feel like throwing the whole current of my life into opposing this giant evil. I don't know but what the religion of Christ de-

mands some such action. (From Frank K. Kelly's *The Martyred Presidents*)

Garfield did "throw the whole current" of his life into the war. In 1862, when Union military victories had been few, he successfully led a brigade of Ohio volunteers against Confederate troops at Middle Creek, Kentucky. At thirty he became a brigadier general—the youngest in the army. Two years later, he was named a major general. In 1863, while still in the army, Garfield was elected to Congress and, on the advice of President Lincoln, resigned his lofty commission and went to Washington, where he served for the next eighteen years.

He became the leading Republican in the House, but many remember him as the man who—right after Lincoln's assassination—stopped a large crowd in New York on their way to get revenge against Southern sympathizers. He had to yell to be heard over the 10,000 rioters, but the crowd quieted and listened as he spoke:

Fellow citizens! Clouds and darkness are round about Him! His pavilion is dark waters and thick clouds of the skies! Judgment and justice are the establishment of

His throne! Mercy and truth shall go before His face! Fellow citizens! God reigns and the government at Washington still lives!

The crowd was reported to be deeply moved by the preacher's admonition. They dispersed without incident.

Garfield proved to be as effective a legislator as he was a speaker. During the Reconstruction Era, he sought to preserve the value of the currency. His dark memories of childhood poverty haunted him, so he worked day and night as a congressman to master a knowledge of economics, trying to find means of helping the many postwar Americans who were crushed under unbelievable poverty. Garfield pushed for rapid industrialization of the nation, believing—successfully—that the productive power of newly invented machines might help produce jobs and plenty for the great multitudes.

Only once was Garfield's reputation tainted; that came through the link with the Credit Mobilier corporation, a Pennsylvania charter that had been found guilty of defrauding the government of millions of dollars while constructing the Union

Pacific Railroad. During the investigation, Oakes Ames, Mobilier lobbyist, claimed
he had slipped stock in the corporation to
Representative Garfield. Garfield did admit
borrowing $329 from Ames (to pay rent
due for his Washington house) but insisted
that the amount had been paid in full.

That link almost ended Garfield's otherwise brilliant career. During his reelection campaign in 1874, Republicans from
his district asked for his resignation, accusing him of taking bribes and going along
with the fraudulent corruption in President Grant's administration. Garfield refused to resign. Instead, he prepared two
pamphlets that answered the two major
accusations against him (his vote for increased congressional salaries and the
transactions with the Credit Mobilier company), and with these pamphlets, he went
from town to town in his district to answer
his wavering public face-to-face. It was a
monumental task and a momumental triumph at the polls.

Six years later, after once again proving
his ability in Congress, he was elected a
United States senator, but he was not
allowed to serve in that office. In one of the
most astounding, ironic Republican con-

ventions, James Abram Garfield was nominated as the 1880 candidate.

Garfield had come to the convention as the head of the Ohio delegation mainly to support his friend John Sherman. The party had split into two factions: the "Stalwarts," headed by New York Senator (and political "boss") Roscoe Conkling, who wanted former President Grant nominated, and the "Half-Breeds," led by Maine Senator James G. Blain. As the convention progressed, some rather unusual political undercurrents became more apparent. Wharton Barker, a political strategist, began implementing a plan to get Garfield nominated. What methods were used, and whether Garfield knew about the plans—both pieces of information have been locked in silence. John Sherman, the candidate from Ohio, knew of the maneuvering at some point, for he wrote, "Whenever the vote of Ohio will be likely to assure the nomination of Garfield, I appeal to every delegate to vote for him. Let Ohio be solid" (quoted from Herbert Eaton's *Presidential Timber*).

Not one vote was cast for him in the first ballot. When on the thirty-third ballot he had one vote, Wharton Barker's plan went into effect. Garfield seemed locked into his destiny, especially when he challenged the thirty-fourth ballot (he had received sixteen votes), saying he had not given consent to be included, but the chairman promptly (and strangely) ruled Garfield out of order.

On the thirty-sixth ballot, Garfield became the undeniable "dark horse" candidate. Another strange, obviously politically motivated, move came when Chester A. Arthur was nominated as Garfield's running mate. Arthur, a man with a questionable record at best, was known to be controlled by Conkling and the powerful New York machine, an "inner circle" that had given new meaning to the phrase "spoils."

In addition to the nagging questions surrounding the 1880 Republican National Convention (Did Garfield know of the undercurrent? Was he "set up" in some diabolical plot?), there were two other less-known "omens." At 1:00 P.M., the hour of the nomination, an eagle landed on Garfield's house in Washington, sat there several minutes, and was seen by many persons (verified by David C. Whitney's *The American President*). Also on the day of his nomination Garfield passed a man distributing leaves of the New Testament. The soon-to-be "last choice" presidential candidate jammed the leaf into his pocket and forgot about it until he was emptying his pockets late that night after the bizarre political turn-around and nomination. The verse that was uppermost when Garfield pulled the leaf from his pocket read:

> What is this then that is written, The stone which the builders rejected, the same is become the head of the corner? (Luke 20:17)

The two signs made such an impression upon Garfield that he mused over them, discussing them with such people as his friend who was the current president, Rutherford B. Hayes.

In the ensuing campaign, Garfield's personal character was savagely attacked; he was accused of being a heavy drinker. But this allegation was disproven. The Credit Mobilier scandal was revived. He was accused of "whitewashing" political frauds. Garfield responded through his "front porch" campaigns, winning the respect of the throngs who visited Washington through his oratory ability, gentle charm (on one occasion, Garfield surprised a large crowd of German-Americans by speaking to them in German), and common sense.

His campaign managers were not so gentle. With a reverse twist on the role of scandalmonger, they disparaged the "exemplary" Democratic candidate, Winfield Scott Hancock, using the media to taint Hancock as primarily motivated by "eating, drinking, and sensual enjoyment." Whether Garfield knew of these remarks is unknown, but—judging from his character—it would seem unlikely that he would have been privy to spreading such slander.

When Americans went to the polls in November, Garfield and Arthur triumphed by a narrow margin, 4,454,416 to 4,444,952 for Hancock and English (an edge of one vote per thousand). Ironically, as Lincoln had been in the previous zero-year election, Garfield was the choice of less than half of the voters who had participated (Iowa's James B. Weaver had drawn votes for his Prohibitionist Party).

One of the Republican "Stalwarts" who amused people by claiming an important role in the victory was Charles J. Guiteau. Guiteau was an ex-evangelist, a failure both as a husband and as a lawyer, a man of sexual irregularities, with a reputation as a swindler and a religious zealot (there is an eternity of difference between religious fervor and Christianity, as there is between true evangelists and warped ideologues like Guiteau). Like Hitler and Jim Jones—extreme, demonic examples of men bidding to use religion or the occult for personal gain and glory—Guiteau was driven by forces that were not of God. Since Guiteau was a staunch Republican like his father (from whom he had received many of his beliefs), he was very interested in the 1880 convention and election.

After Garfield's nomination, Guiteau decided to give up his other "professions" and donate his talents to the Republican cause. He wrote a speech endorsing Garfield, then tried to become a paid speaker, but Garfield's officials were not impressed with either Guiteau or his speech. Not one to give up so easily, Guiteau had his speech printed, passed out as many copies as he could, and then lauded himself for the "important role" he had played when Garfield won the close decision over Hancock. As a reward, he felt entitled to a government position; during Guiteau's visit in Washington after the inauguration, Garfield listened politely as Guiteau asked for the position as consul in Paris, but he made no promises to the man, who had become something of a joke and nuisance.

By May, 1881, Guiteau had become such a pest through his daily attempts to talk to high officials that the White House was ordered not to admit "that man." Enraged over the rebuff, the disappointed office seeker called the president a traitor to "the men that made him." After a major faction in the Republican Party (the "Stalwarts" and "Half-Breeds" again), Charles Guiteau hatched the idea of killing President Garfield, rationalizing that the leader "who had forgotten the little people" was a madman who was intent on destroying the nation. Guiteau therefore reasoned that Garfield's removal would be:

> an act of God. . . . After praying for two weeks, this [the assassination] had been a direct inspiration from the Deity. (Quoted from *The Life and Letters of James Abram Garfield*, volume two, by Theodore Clarke Smith)

The truth was, of course, that the president was well on the way to becoming known as a champion of the common people (his first act after being sworn into office was to kiss his aged mother and thank her for her encouragement and support). He stood victorious in a face-off with Conkling's corrupt machine. Within weeks afer his inauguration (March 4, 1881), he was already winning back for the Presidency a measure of prestige it had lost since Lincoln's assassination and the chaos that followed. In foreign affairs, Garfield directed his secretary of state to invite all of the American republics to a conference that would meet in Washington in 1882. It was an unprecedented move, one aimed at international diplomacy, but the conference never took place.

Maybe Garfield had a premonition of his own death. On June 30, 1881, Garfield sent for Robert Lincoln, the son of the late president, and asked him to recount all his memories of the assassination of his famous father. Lincoln talked for more than an hour while the president listened intently.

On July 2, 1881, two days later, en route to make a speech at Williams College, Garfield stood at the Washington railway depot, talking and laughing with Secretary of State James Blaine. As he did, Charles Jules Guiteau (who had been foiled three times before), stepped behind him. In an instant (Where were the President's guards?), Guiteau's English "bulldog" pistol had barked (he had selected a particularly fancy revolver because it would look good in a museum someday!). As he fired the gun, he swore, "I am a Stalwart and now Arthur is president!"

"My God, what is this?" cried the stricken president as he slumped to the ground. Guiteau replied by calmly firing a second bullet, which passed harmlessly through the fallen leader's sleeve.

When the police did close in on the assassin, Guiteau did not resist. He carried a letter in his pocket:

> To the White House: The President's tragic death was a sad necessity but it will unite the Republican Party and save the Republic. Life is a flimsy dream, and it matters little when one goes. A human life is of small value. During the war, thousands of brave boys went down without a tear.
>
> I presume the President was a Christian and that he will be happier in Paradise than here. It will be no worse for Mrs. Garfield, dear soul, to part with her husband this way than by natural death. He is liable to go any time, anyway.
>
> I have no ill will toward the President. His death was a political necessity. I am a

lawyer, a theologian, and a politician. I am a stalwart of the stalwarts. I was with General Grant and the rest of our men during the canvass. . . . I have some papers for the Press. . . . I am going to jail. (From *The Martyred Presidents*)

Amid a throng frozen with horror, the president lay in a dark red pool of blood. In the frantic pandemonium, a call for assistance was heard by Dr. Smith Townsend. Soon other doctors (C.B. Purvis and D. Willard Bliss) arrived on the scene. The president was deathly pale and vomiting. He was not expected to live the night. A well-documented diary written by Jim, the president's son, graphically recalls the accounts of that day:

July 2, 1881. I rose at 7 and went into Papa's room and talked till 8. . . . We all started for the depot [sons Hal and Jim in a second carriage] to go on the trip to Williamstown. When we arrived at the depot we found Papa had been shot by a man named Guiteau. I was frightened and could do nothing but cry. Hal was very brave and helped. He [the president] was very dangerously wounded. He was very weak at first but revived and was taken home [to the White House] at 10 o'clock and Mamma was dispatched for [she was in Elberon, New Jersey]. . . . At 6 Mamma. . . arrived. Mamma was very brave and courageous. Papa was expected to die within an hour at 7 . . . At 9 the reaction commenced and hope revived a little . . . I went in and watched him a little while and he told me "to keep up my pluck" and said that "the upper story was not hurt it was the hull." Mamma's arrival seemed to encourage him a great deal. The doctor said that there was one chance in 1000 and he said "I will take that one" . . . We go to bed with some hope.

For seventy-nine days James A. Garfield clung to life. The superficial arm wound healed quickly, but the bullet in his back proved troublesome. A mob of doctors poked and probed the president with unclean instruments that increased the infection. In the weeks that followed, as the president grew worse, well-wishers from all over the nation brought a variety of medicines, quack formulas, and apparatuses to help their beloved leader recover.

Dr. Bliss selected three physicians (from the countless who offered advice): Dr. Robert Reyburn, Surgeon General Joseph K. Barnes, and Surgeon J.J. Woodward (Little had Woodward or Barnes realized sixteen years before—as they examined President Lincoln—that they would once more work together on a president who would be the victim of an assassination. Or was it mere coincidence? What was behind their dismissal from the case near the end of the president's life?).

The probings and supposed medical blunders were questionable from the start. Even with medicine as it was in 1881, many people lived with similar wounds and recovered nicely. Leading physicians of the time were astounded at the reported ineptness of the doctors:

> From an antiseptic view, we might criticize the introduction of the fingers of several surgeons into the wound. . .not in accord with the prevailing present theories . . . (Boston's Dr. J. Collins Warren [1881 issue of the *Boston Medical and Surgical Journal*])

> It is indeed humiliating to the historian to record such a mass of irretrievable blunders. . .the repeated introduction of fingers, probes and catheters . . . (Dr. M. Schuppert [1881 issue of *Gaillard's Medical Journal*])

> The damage which proceeds from a bullet is caused by it in its course; the

damage which is added to it mostly pro-
ceeds from the examiner's fingers. If they
had entirely omitted the search after the
bullet and immediately after injury dressed
the wound in a real antispetic way, the
President might perhaps still be alive. . . .
It seems that the attending physicians
were under the pressure of public opinion
that they were doing far too little, but
according to my opinion they have not
done too little but far too much. (Dr.
Friedrich Esmarch, Professor of Surgery
at the University of Kiel, Germany [quoted
from an editorial in an 1882 *Boston Medical and Surgical Journal*])

Summing up the case from an allopathic
standpoint, the man is ignorantly or will-
fully blind who fails to see that President
Garfield's case has been the most grossly
mismanaged case in modern history, and
his surgeons are guilty of deliberate attempt
to throw the burden of a glaring incompet-
ency upon Providence, rather than leave it
where it justly belongs. (Dr. J.A. Gilchrist
[*Medical Counselor*, October 19, 1881])

Historians have tried to be kind to the
attending physicians, but the questions
have continued to plague medical research-
ers. Many feel that if President Garfield
had been made (or allowed) to get up and

walk around, taking in sunshine and fresh air (he did have feeling in his lower extremities, and some observers feel that he should not have been assigned paraplegic status), his strong body might have recovered.

But all the questions (and answers) are theoretical. The president lingered on through the hot summer, and on September 6 he was moved in a specially equipped train to Francklyn Cottage in Elberon, New Jersey. His wife constantly attended him and prepared all his meals. He seemed to be recovering until September 19, when he awoke with a chill. During the day he became progressively weaker.

Just two days before the president had asked a friend, "Do you think my name will have a place in human history?" To which the friend answered, "Yes, a grand one, but a grander one in human hearts. You must not talk that way. You have a great work yet to perform."

Garfield replied, "No, my work is done."

This great man who loved poetry, his family, his country, and—most of all—the Christ he had often preached about and spoken to, died at 10:30 P.M. on September 19. He was the second president in twenty years to be murdered while in office, and the third zero-year president in a row to die. His remains (minus several vertebrae which were used both for research and for an exhibit in his assassin's trial) were buried in Cleveland.

Less than a month later "one of the most spectacular trials in American history" began. It lasted eleven weeks. Like a nightmarish circus, the courtroom was filled with jeering spectators and Guiteau's vile outbursts. One of the more macabre touches came when the assassin reportedly handled Garfield's vertebrae in the courtroom. On January 25, 1881, the trial ended. It took the jury less than an hour's deliberation to find Guiteau guilty.

On June 30, 1882, the bearded, tragic, twisted forty-year-old man was led to the gallows before a crowd of Washington spectators (many of whom had paid exorbitant prices to see the execution). On the platform Guiteau began reciting a poem he had written especially for the occasion:

> I saved my party and my land;
> Glory Hallelujah!
> But they have murdered me for it
> And that is the reason
> I am going to the Lordy.

Glory Hallelujah! Glory Hallelujah!

He continued shouting "glory" (the one thing that had eluded him all his life) even as the black hood was pulled over his face. In an instant, the oldest man ever to kill an American president was dead—launched on an eternal trajectory to an unknown fate.

It is understandable, but nonetheless it remains a paradox, that President Garfield should be known as little more than a man who was shot by a demented office seeker. He could have been the Christian president who would have altered the direction and destiny of the people who elected him. Saddened Americans would soon forget his moral courage and remember only the assassination.

If the assassination and medical problems were part of a larger plot to replace Garfield with Roscoe Conkling's handpicked associate, Chester A. Arthur, and spread the powerful New York spoils system across the nation, the plot had misfired. Chester Arthur fooled everyone— friends and enemies alike—by turning against his "boss," changing from a petty politician into a man sincerely dedicated to the good of the country. He was courageous, even when he completely lost the support of his former political bosses. Henry Ward Beecher once remarked about Garfield's successor, "I can hardly imagine how he could have done better."

Maybe there was no diabolical plot executed by human marionettes. Then why the ominous cloud of doom that seemed to hang over the last three presidents elected during the zero year? It seemed more than mere coincidence when such a terrible thing happened to that gentle man of God elected in 1880, but the answers have remained hypothetical and hopeless, seemingly unrelated segments in *The Presidential Zero-Year Mystery.*

5

William McKinley—
Damaging Doubts

We are all going . . . we are all going . . . (President McKinley's last words, September 14, 1901)

William McKinley was one of the few men who were candid enough to admit to their presidential aspirations. He openly sought the office (1888 and 1892) and was successful twice (1896 and 1900—both times a winner over the Democrat William Jennings Bryan). He was also a curious mix of genuine Christianity and money-controlled, smoke-filled-room politics.

When reelected at the turn of the century, he was president of a country that was caught at a crossroads. Only a few years before the last organized Indian battle had taken place at Wounded Knee, South Dakota (December 29, 1890). That primitive world seemed so far away in 1900, as Americans discovered the mobility of automobiles, bicycles, and affordable railway trips. Even the temperance advocate Carry A. Nation, with her saloon-wrecking hatchet, the pre-Azusa Street Pentecostal movements, and such rising "sawdust trail" evangelists as Bob Jones, Gypsy Smith, and Dwight L. Moody could not seem to turn America's attention from a preoccupation with amusements (Edison's first "motion pictures" were seen in New York during 1896), games (especially baseball), and frolic that had developed during the "Gay Nineties." People longed to forget the past, especially the 1893 Depression.

McKinley's career had mirrored the growing pains of the entire nation. He had reached the top elected position with the powerful backing of Marcus Alonzo (Mark) Hanna, the shrewd financier, trusts "boss," and political kingmaker. Hanna had not only "overseen" McKinley's presidential aspirations but had rescued him from financial disaster. Yet in the midst of obvious political double-dealing, William McKinley was a throwback to men of a gentler, less troublesome time.

Born in Niles, Ohio, on January 29, 1843,

William was born the seventh in a family of nine children. His father was absent on business (iron manufacturing) during much of his youth, so young William was quite influenced by his mother, Nancy Allison McKinley, especially by her strong Christian faith. When William was nine, his family moved to Poland, Ohio, where he and the other McKinley youngsters attended Union Seminary, a small private school. There he became involved both in oratory and the local Methodist Church, so much so that his mother hoped he would become a minister. This was not his personal desire, but his strong Christian beliefs that could have helped him be a successful clergyman proved to be part of the outstanding character he exhibited.

He attended Allegheny College in Meade, Pennsylvania, for a brief time, then returned home to recuperate from an illness and to help the struggling family. He was teaching in a country school when the Civil War broke out. Enlisting as a private in the Union Army, he served heroically and at the end of the war was mustered out as a brevet major of volunteers. Throughout the war he was known for his moral example. Even as thousands of Union men died from diseases such as typhoid fever, McKinley enjoyed excellent health. Col. Rutherford Hayes, who later became president, noticed him and wrote: "McKinley is one of the finest, bravest officers in the army" (quoted from *The Martyred Presidents*).

Like Lincoln, McKinley shared the belief that the war was a crusade to save the Union, and that God would bring the war to an end when the nation had suffered enough.

And like Lincoln, McKinley decided to study law. After attending law school in Albany, New York, he was admitted to the bar in March, 1867, and started his practice soon afterwards in Canton, Ohio. He fell in love with Ida Saxton, the beautiful daughter of Canton's leading banker, James Saxton—a man who had "clout" throughout the state.

On January 25, 1871, Ida and William were married. He was twenty-eight; she was twenty-two. Within five years she lost both her mother and two baby daughters. That, coupled with Mrs. McKinley's reported obsession that caused her to believe these calamities were payments of past sins (his or hers), so shattered her nervous system that she developed epilepsy and for the rest of her life could not tell from minute to minute when she would fall unconscious. With a patience and kindness rarely exhibited—then or now—McKinley watched over her and insisted that she go everywhere with him. From that point he gave up his only diversions, walking and horseback riding, and even curtailed his working hours so he could be with her. The unusual love and allegiance forged by mutual sorrow and the sick wife's complete emotional dependence on her husband would be binding for their twenty-six remaining years together.

In 1877, McKinley won a seat in Congress. His attractive personality, exemplary character, and quick intelligence enabled him to rise rapidly. Economically and politically he was a conservative, yet he was noted as a progressive. During his fourteen years in the House, he became a leading Republican.

1892 marked the year that McKinley returned to Ohio as governor of the state. His slogan, "Regular employment, good wages, and education bring prosperity," was part of the election campaign, but the most potent force was Hanna's backing. McKinley had talked about running for president of the United States but was discouraged from doing so by Mark Hanna. The time was not yet right.

In 1893, McKinley was reelected as governor. His own fortune was wiped out during the 1893 Depression by the failure of a business partner, but friends (especially one man in particular) came to his rescue and paid the $100,000 debt. In spite of his problems, his love for Ida remained constant, even though she had—for all practical purposes—become an invalid. Reports of his devotion were well-known. Every afternoon during his reign as governor, he would interrupt whatever business he was engaged in to step to the window of his office and wave a handkerchief to his wife, who was waiting for the greeting from their hotel suite across the street from his office. Every morning after leaving the hotel, he was known to pause outside, remove his hat, and bow to her at the window before proceeding to his office.

He was a good governor, serving for two terms. During his last term, Mark Hanna retired from his own business enterprises and began putting together the machine necessary to get McKinley nominated for the 1896 presidential election. Money was no handicap, and Hanna was so effective that McKinley was nominated on the first ballot at the St. Louis Republican National Convention.

The campaign of 1896 had to be one of the most dramatic in the history of the United States. William Jennings Bryan, the thirty-six-year-old "Boy Orator of the Platte," attacked the trusts and Wall Street, sweeping the Democratic convention into a fever of excitement. He was chosen to oppose McKinley and began verbal blasts at the Republicans, picturing the GOP candidate and the multimillionaire Hanna as tools of big business, declaring that the small people of America had been forgotten.

Bryan made a gallant fight, but he had terrible handicaps. He was young, brash, and relatively unknown. Business leaders reacted to him like they would have reacted to a plague (more than a few workers across the nation received silent notices in their pay envelopes—warnings that their job would be gone if Bryan was elected).

Whether McKinley was aware of the political games being played around him is unclear. Perhaps he was poignantly naive, but that seems unusual considering the legislative arenas he had been accustomed to. He remained calm, delivering his campaign speeches to audiences (thanks to Hanna's free train rides, he made a whirlwind tour through seventeen states) and resting upon his belief that he would win if it was God's will.

In the November election, McKinley's margin over Bryan was narrow in the popular vote and 271 to 176 in the electoral college. As the returns came in, clubs and hotels were packed with celebrating merchants, bankers, and businessmen. McKinley, however, knelt at his cottage in Canton, one arm holding his aged mother, the other around his trembling wife, as his mother prayed a simple prayer: "Oh, God, keep him humble." Somehow for McKinley, that moment epitomized his life—reverent calmness in spite of the chaotic environment.

McKinley's first term was marked by a 100-day war with Spain (1898), the most brief, most unique and most one-sided war that America ever fought. McKinley didn't want war, especially a war that seemed planned to fill businessmen's and publishers' coffers. (It still seems suspicious that the outgoing President Cleveland would remark to McKinley, "I am deeply sorry, Mr. President, to pass on to you a war with Spain. It will come within two years. Nothing can stop it.") Nonetheless, it was successful (and profitable for some).

Also, during the first term, McKinley was saddened by the death of his vice president, Garret A. Hobart, in November of 1899.

In a dubious attempt to placate American imperialists, McKinley tabbed the Spanish-American war hero, Teddy Roosevelt, to be his running mate for the 1900 bid. Despite the Democrat Bryan's brilliant attempt, the McKinley/Roosevelt team again won by a comfortable margin. There had been talk about the zero-year death cycle that had haunted Harrison, Lincoln, and Garfield, but it was either ignored or forgotten as the second term progressed pleasantly and uneventfully.

Then it happened. McKinley left Washington for Buffalo on September 5, 1901. The Pan American Exposition was not faring as well in attendance as had been hoped, so McKinley was asked to make an appearance (and address) to bolster the effort.

On September 6, the day after his speech in Buffalo, the president stood shaking hands (he was famous for his "fifty-a-minute" handshake routine). Earlier, George Cortelyou, the president's secretary, had canceled the handshaking plans, thinking it impossible to effectively protect the chief executive (or was it some premonition?), but he was overruled. On hand were approximately sixty guards, but the security was below par even by the standards of that day. The Secret Service men, who should have been standing next to the president, were several feet away. George Cortelyou seemed to be the only one concerned. It was 4:00 P.M., and the line was moving rapidly. A twenty-eight-year-old ex-factory worker and farmhand named Leon Czolgosz moved toward McKinley with his right hand wrapped in a bandage. As he advanced toward the front of the line, a Secret Service agent reportedly touched his shoulder and asked, "Hurt your hand?" When Czolgosz nodded, the agent directed him to a first-aid station. Czolgosz shook his head, "Later. After I meet the president. I've been waiting a long time."

As he approached the chief executive,

Czolgosz apologized for the bandage, shook left hands, and moved on. After several more citizens extended their greetings, Czolgosz stepped up again. As Secret Service agent Samuel Ireland grabbed Czolgosz's shoulder to move him along quickly, a .32-caliber Iver Johnson revolver roared from the handkerchief. Once. Twice. The president stood bewildered, then slumped, whispering to his secretary, "My wife—be careful, Cortelyou, how you tell her—oh, be careful." Even in that moment he was concerned about Ida—and even about his assassin ("Don't let them hurt him" or, depending upon which historian one is reading, "Be easy with him, boys.").

The fallen president was whisked to the Exposition hospital. Considering all the facets of the case, the McKinley operation might well rank as one of the most dramatic and controversial surgical procedures ever performed in the United States. Dr. Matthew Mann was the presiding surgeon.

"Thy kingdom come, thy will be done," murmured the fallen leader as he went unconscious from the ether administered to him. For the greater part of two hours,

Mann worked, unsuccessfully, using the only instruments "available" from another doctor's pocket case (which did not contain a contractor, even if the fatal bullet had been found). Mysteriously, in the next room, unnoticed by all until the operation was virtually over, was another doctor's complete set of surgical instruments. Another note of consternation was the physicians' refusal to utilize the newly discovered X-ray equipment. Later there would be a semantic difference of opinion between the attending doctors concerning the methods used and the ensuing infection.

On September 13, the president, his condition worsening, sensed the end was near and asked the doctors to pray with him. He recited the Lord's Prayer. Then when Mrs. McKinley entered the room, and as she embraced her devoted husband, he moved his lips to speak: "Goodbye—goodbye, all. . . . His will, not ours, be done." Fainter and fainter the words came as he mouthed his favorite hymn:

Nearer, my God, to Thee,
   Nearer to Thee!
E'en though it be a cross . . .

There was a moment of silence, then he

murmured, "That has been my inextinguishable prayer. It is God's way" (quoted from *Our Murdered Presidents*). He lapsed into a coma, murmuring only once more to Ida, then at 2:15 A.M., on Saturday, September 14, he was pronounced dead.

The similarities between the third and fourth zero-year presidents are strange. Both Garfield and McKinley were from Ohio. Both presidents died in September. Both had been shot twice from a close range, yet in each instance only one of the two shots was fatal (both of the other bullets caused only superficial damage). For both, the actual position of the lethal bullet remained a mystery to both assemblages of doctors. The most striking similarity was their shared belief in a personal Savior, Jesus Christ.

There was one major difference—Garfield languished for eighty days, but McKinley lived for only eight days. The medical puzzles as they tottered between death and life were part of the total mystery and would provide material for many medical school debates.

Like John Booth and Charles Guiteau before him, Leon F. Czolgosz expressed no remorse for his infamous crime. He went on trial September 23, 1901. The trial lasted eight hours and twenty-six minutes, a kangaroo court that featured an unprepared defense. Leon received the guilty verdict without showing any sign of emotion.

As he sat in the electric chair in Auburn State Prison on October 29, 1901, Czolgosz said, "I killed the president because he was the enemy of the good people—the good working people. I am not sorry for my crime." Shortly after 7:00 A.M. he was dead. Sulfuric acid was poured into his coffin to decompose his body within twelve hours— a tragic eulogy for a tragic, twisted life.

Mixed with the sorrow of the people of the United States was a wave of humiliation that such a terrible record of assassinations could exist in America.

Though Leon Czolgosz was lowered into a hastily dug prison grave, and despite the fact that William McKinley's coffin was laid to its final rest in Canton's West Lawn Cemetery, questions have continued to plague investigative historians. The extensive autopsy of the chief executive yielded more puzzles than peace, especially concerning the surgery and medical practices.

But once again, the leader was dead. The

question "why?" seems almost unnecessary. Maybe all of the irregularities in Buffalo were unrelated incidents leading to the same quizzical tragedy. Maybe not.

If there was some sort of a secret conspiracy, it certainly was a political blunder of sorts; McKinley's successor, Theodore Roosevelt, was known as a champion of the people, a "trust buster," and a no-nonsense leader in world relations.

It can be frustrating to attempt to find the "hidden picture." Perhaps none even existed, but the doubts that continue to surround the McKinley assassination are just one more eerie installment in *The Presidential Zero-Year Mystery*.

6

Warren Gamaliel Harding—
Out of His Place

I was quite reluctant to get into the presidential game but I came to find out that a man in public life cannot always map out his way according to his own preferences. Therefore, I decided to go in and do the best that I could, under more or less difficult circumstances. (President Harding [quoted from *The Available Man*])

Once, when disciplining young Warren for some minor offense, the future president's weary father reportedly said, "I guess I ought to be thankful you're a boy. If you'd been a girl, every young scalawag in town would have had his way with you by now!"

After becoming President of the United States, Harding was quoted as having reiterated that statement: "It is a good thing I am not a woman. I would always be pregnant. I cannot say no."

During the period between his father's statement and Harding's own admission that it was true, one of Harding's college classmates once said, "The difference between you and George Washington is he couldn't tell a lie, and you can't tell a liar!"

Those three statements capsulize—in a small way—the life, career and death of America's twenty-ninth president—and the subsequent scandals connected to his administration. He was softhearted to a fault, said to believe that there could not be evil in any man, yet his administration and personal reputation were riddled—at least in part—with corruption and sensual scandal.

When he said, "We mean to have less of government in business and more business in government," in his campaign speeches, little did the country know what kind of sizzling "business" would be taking place. Likewise, little did the country know what twist of ironic fate would once again claim the 1920 zero-year president—while in office. Under better conditions, or had he openly been assassinated, he might have

been another McKinley-type or Garfield-
type hero; unfortunately, a bizarre chain
of events caused him to be regarded as one
of the worst presidents in America's history. In truth, he was neither as guilty nor
as unblemished as he has been described
by various historians.

The first of George and Phoebe Harding's eight children, Warren was born on
November 2, 1865, on a farm in Morrow
County in north central Ohio. Like any
other farm boy, his life was filled with
chores; unlike most other boys, Warren's
father was a practitioner of homeopathic
medicine, so Warren sometimes accompanied his father on horse-and-buggy calls.

Religion was very, very important in
the Harding household, as was education.
"Winnie" (a nickname given Warren by his
mother) was heavily influenced during the
early years by his father's staunch Baptist
heritage, his mother's Methodist (and later
Seventh-Day Adventist) zeal, and the no-
nonsense experiences in a nearby country
school his grandfather had built.

Unfounded, but persistent, rumors in
his hometown purported that the Harding
family was "tainted by nigger blood"

(seemingly the ultimate insult in Blooming Grove, Ohio, during his childhood days) left a mark of inferiority that taunted him the rest of his life (Harding was, in fact, light haired with blue eyes).

When he was ten, he became a printer's apprentice in the office of a local newspaper, the *Caldonia Argus*—a move that would heavily influence Harding's next decades in newspaper work.

At fourteen, despite the family's shaky financial status, Harding was allowed to enter Iberia College (tuition was a whopping seven dollars a term). That year— 1880—was politically explosive for all the students at Iberia, since it was at the height of the Garfield-Hancock campaigns. Though in the minority, Harding became an outspoken Republican.

Harding continued his interest in newspaper work through his two years in college, working at the Union *Register*, then beginning the Iberia *Spectator*, a college paper (Harding wrote in one editorial, "The *Spectator* is taken by every family in our city excepting a few stingy old grumblers who take no more interest in home enterprise than a mule takes in a hive of bees"—quoted from Francis Russell's

The Shadow of Blooming Grove).

Harding was one of three Iberia graduates during 1882. A month prior to his graduation (Warren's commencement address was entitled, "It Can Never Be Rubbed Out"), Harding's parents moved to Marion, the county seat, some nine miles away from Blooming Grove. After aborted attempts at teaching and insurance selling, Harding returned to a newspaper career, working first as a reporter for one of the town's three publications (Marion had a population of four thousand at that time).

Soon, with two associates, he bought the *Star*, a mortgaged paper, for three hundred dollars, and at the age of nineteen began a business as a newspaper proprietor. Regardless of the taunts that have since been leveled at the young entrepreneur, Harding's success was certainly from the Horatio Alger mold. He started with nothing but dreams, and through boasting, bluffing, and "elbow grease," he turned a dying rag into a powerful small-town newspaper. He was fortunate to be able to buy at the right time (since Marion doubled in population during the first decade he owned the *Star*), but Harding was also a total believer in and example of the self-made man. However crafty his methods were in business, he felt "the ends justified the means" and were virtuous if they provided jobs and wealth.

Yet to type him as being crafty is a partial misjudgment. He was also extremely kind and sympathetic. In thirty-six years as publisher of the Marion *Star*, he was said to have never dismissed a single employee. He was conscious of the image of his city, a lifetime promoter of the small town (among other civic affairs, W.G.—as his friends affectionately called him—reorganized a local cornet group into a lively and professional ensemble, "The Marion People's Band").

1886 marked his definite entry into politics. Warren became involved in James G. Blaine's ill-fated attempt to dethrone Grover Cleveland. He took the defeat of "the plumed knight" personally and resolved to enter politics to a greater extent.

In 1891, at the age of twenty-six, he was on his way to becoming Marion's leading citizen. He married Florence DeWolfe Kling, a thirty-year-old divorcee (also, incidentally, the daughter of the wealthiest man in Marion). Flossie (to her friends), or the "Duchess" (to W.G.), had been deserted by her husband and disowned by her father. A cold, imperious woman, she soon took over the business side of running the Marion *Star*, became the driving force behind Harding's business career, and became the domineering power in his political pushes. Unfortunately, Harding's first attempt to win public office ended in defeat (his 1892 bid for county auditor), but the husband/wife team was undaunted. By the end of the 1890s the *Star* had become a financial success and an influential voice in Republican Party affairs, and in 1899 Harding won the election for the Ohio state senate.

On the surface he was a typical "Main Streeter" at the turn of the century, genial and easy-going, a dedicated family man, and a charming "joiner." In truth, his marriage seemed to be only a working relationship with an ambitious woman who was involved with astrology and possibly the occult. It is reported that, over a period of fifteen years, he was involved in a passionate love affair with the wife of a good friend. In truth, despite his surface calmness, Harding suffered serious breakdowns in times of stress (he was only twenty-two when he suffered his first nervous breakdown and was hospitalized in a sanitarium; he had four similar episodes over the next twelve years).

In 1909, after serving two terms as state senator and one term as lieutenant governor of Ohio, Harding won the Republican nomination for governor. Although he lost the election, his campaign was managed by Harry M. Daugherty, a sharp-eyed politician. That relationship was to prove to be one of the most influential in Harding's climb from Marion's whispered-about hero to United States senator (1914).

Harding served in Washington mostly as a prelude in the Duchess-and-Daugherty plan for the Presidency. In reality, his term as a United States lawmaker was as undistinguished as his governmental positions in Ohio had been. He introduced no measures of great significance. His own colleagues pointed to his lack of deep convictions. On the two great issues of the day (on which he had to take some semblance of a stand), he voted for prohibition (though he was known as a hearty drinker) and for women's suffrage (though he was quoted as doubting the wisdom of letting women vote).

Also of note is the fact that he failed to

answer nearly half of the roll calls. After reading reams of exposé material written by everyone from intimates to colleagues, there is little doubt that a portion of Harding's time was taken up with less-than-honorable pursuits.

He was a well-built six-footer with the tanned face, elegant bearing, and speaking voice of a matinee idol. Though the reports were successfully muted for some time, he also seemed to have an affinity for the gentler sex, most notably Nan Britton, a blonde nearly thirty years his junior. Miss Britton had helped at the *Star* as a teenager, had fastened her attentions on the handsome editor, and was obsessed (without his knowledge) with romantic aspirations toward him until two years after he entered the Senate. After she wrote a letter to Harding, he arranged for a job for her in New York, met her frequently in New York and Washington, and took his "niece" on trips away from the jealous eyes of the Duchess. On October 22, 1919, Nan gave birth to a daughter (Elizabeth Ann Harding) in Asbury Park, New Jersey.

With all the fun it is alleged that he enjoyed, it is not unusual that he was not entirely enthusiastic when Daugherty "urged" him to run for president in 1920. Daugherty (perhaps alone) also came up with a plan to promote his protégé to the nation's highest office.

The 1920 Republican convention shaped up as a fight between General Leonard Wood and Frank Lowden, governor of Illinois. After a long list of other possible Republican contenders, Senator Harding's name was also mentioned. One evening at that Republican convention in Chicago will always hold special significance in history. The tight race between the two leading contenders induced a group of powerful men (Col. George Harvey, Sen. Henry Cabot Lodge, Sen. Charles Curtis, Sen. Frank Brandegee, and eleven other prominent individuals met in the Blackstone Hotel) to endorse Harding as a third candidate. One man not present had been quoted by a *New York Times* reporter as saying:

> I don't expect Senator Harding to be nominated on the first, second, or third ballots, but I think we can afford to take chances that about eleven minutes after two, Friday morning of the convention, when fifteen or twenty weary men are sitting around a table, someone will say "Who will we nominate?" At that decisive mo-

ment the friends of Harding will suggest him and we can well afford to abide by the result.

Harry Micajah Daugherty proved to be an amazing prophet. The evening came off almost exactly as he had predicted (or at least the way the reporter had printed his prediction), even to the bleary-eyed leaders in the smoke-filled room at 2:11 A.M.

Harding was stunned, especially when his name appeared on the eighth ballot and when he won the Republican nomination for president on the tenth.

Harding had insisted on staying in the Senate, but Daugherty knew he had Mrs. Harding on his side. She had already been told by a fortuneteller that she would someday be the first lady. Her interest in the occult had been stimulated initially in Washington by a clairvoyant named Madame Marcia, who reportedly first won Mrs. Harding's confidence with a character profile of the senator based upon the time of his birth. Given that information, the seeress proclaimed him thus:

Sympathetic, kindly, intuitive, free with promises and trustful of friends; enthusiastic, impulsive. Perplexed over financial affairs. Many clandestine love affairs; inclined to recurrent moods of melancholia. (Quoted from *Scandals in the Highest Office*)

Based upon that "truth," Mrs. Harding consulted many seers during her remaining years in Washington, allegedly becoming increasingly reliant upon clairvoyants, believing—based upon the information— that her husband's calling was to be Chief Executive. Therefore, Daugherty had little trouble enlisting her assistance (one point of contention arises—"Who actually enlisted whom?"), and together the two "persuaded" Harding to enter the nomination ring.

With "Normalcy for the Nation" as his theme, Harding led a comfortable, uninteresting compaign, mainly from the front porch of his Marion home. Despite a few sensational reflections on his wayward flirtations and bloodline, Americans seemed to like the change Harding represented. The people were tired of government restrictions and hardships of war (all attributed to the Democrats) and wanted a new administration to bring back the "good ol' days."

Harding won the election over Democratic nominee James M. Cox by more than 60 percent of the popular vote. This landslide victory in the electoral college was the largest margin ever achieved up to that point in history.

As in all moments of great victory, depths followed shortly. He was, at best, a political figurehead. He knew he was out of place— "I am not fit for this office and never should have been here." His wife knew his inadequacies—once she was overheard by a White House secretary who heard the first lady challenge her husband, "Well, Warren Harding, I have got you the Presidency; what are you going to do with it?"

What he *did* was a travesty, for he did so very little. What his intimates did was even more of a travesty.

Before his nomination, he declared:

America's present need is not heroics, but healing; not nostrums, but normalcy; not revolution, but restoration; not agitation, but adjustment; not surgery, but serenity; not the dramatic, but the dispassionate; not experiment, but equipoise; not submergence in internationality, but sustainment in triumphant nationality.

While semantic murkiness (plus powerful friends making the right decisions) did get him to the highest office, semantics did not suffice to sustain him in executive success.

The new president and first lady got off to a popular start by ordering the White House gates to be opened (they had been closed during Woodrow Wilson's illness) and public tours reinstated. As president, his small-town habits remained: playing poker most nights with his closest friends, shooting in the mid-nineties on the links, and taking in baseball games (Babe Ruth was in his prime then). He also liked horseback riding. He and the Duchess attended the Calvary Baptist Church fairly regularly.

He named some highly able men to his Cabinet, but many of his friends used their official positions to pad their pockets. (One example, Albert Fall, was convicted. As Harding's secretary of the interior, he accepted a $100,000 bribe for leasing United States oil reserves to private interests.) As scandals increased, with possibly millions of dollars involved, Harding's "more business in government" certainly received new meanings. Some historians have pointed to Harding's innocence, explaining he did not know what was going on. That innocence was not reflected in Harding's worried muttering, "My friends, they're the ones that keep me walking the floors nights!"

In truth, Harding did know. After the scandal began to grow, and after several mysterious suicides occurred, Harding became worried.

At this time his valet, Arthur Brooks, had a premonition of something happening to Harding. A clairvoyant warned Mrs. Harding of dark clouds over the president. By June, 1923, he was admonished to set out on a "voyage of understanding" that would take him across the continent to Alaska. Throughout the "voyage" Harding was despondent and ill. From that point on, the details of his life become clouded, secretive, and mysterious.

It is known that somewhere between Alaska and Seattle an airplane delivered special mail that included a coded message. Was it information about more scandals? Was it warnings to keep quiet?

One thing is known for sure—he did know of the irregularities, and he certainly did not "blow the whistle." His secretary of commerce, Herbert Hoover, had urged him to expose the scandals to the unknowing public, but Harding seemingly feared something or someone.

Whatever was in the message was hard-striking. He collapsed shortly after receiving it. His physician, Surgeon General Charles Sawyer, at first diagnosed his condition as indigestion caused by tainted crab meat. Other reports referred to a heart attack. He seemed to be recovering by July 29 when he arrived in San Francisco, but then "pneumonia" was reported. Again the president seemed to be recovering, when—alone with Mrs. Harding in a motel room—at 7:32 P.M., on August 2, 1923, everybody's "second choice" died.

He was the fifth zero-year president in succession to die while in office. The circumstances surrounding his death remain as mysterious as they were with the others.

The Duchess refused to allow an autopsy. She refused to have a death mask made. The official cause—according to Dr. Sawyer—was a cerebral hemorrhage (thrombosis). For some reason, the president's body was embalmed almost immediately.

This plunged the nation into mourning. Throughout the ordeal, Mrs. Harding's composure was surprising; nobody saw her shed a tear. In short order, she and

Daugherty destroyed ledger sheets, bank records, and correspondence. Washington (and God only knows where else) became a montage of erased trails.

Rumors began floating about murder and suicide. Conspiracy was supposed to have put Harding in the White House to begin with (this was becoming common knowledge by 1923); was it any less logical that some conspiracy would have done away with a despondent president that some were afraid would break and "tell everything he knew"? Who knows? Perhaps his death resulted from logical natural causes.

Post-mortem incidents posed further questions. Daugherty, in his book *The Inside Story of the Harding Tragedy*, raised more questions about the mysterious suicides, affairs, and the ill-timed death of his protégé. He knew more than he told.

Dr. Sawyer, the physician who certified Harding's cause of death as thrombosis, died unexpectedly one year later of the same cause. Mrs. Harding, for some reason, was present at Dr. Sawyer's death, too. A half year later Mrs. Harding died.

These deaths, the circumstances, the real stories—seem reminiscent of the conclusion of a Shakespearean tragedy. Why was Harding the only one poisoned by the crab meat when it was served to everybody in the party? Why had Mrs. Harding refused an autopsy? Why was she incredibly composed at the funeral? How much did she know—about her husband's wayward tendencies and his corrupt administration?

Among most historians there is agreement that everything was not told. Was it murder, suicide, or did everything happen as certified? Did President Harding know he would most certainly be impeached within the coming year?

Despite these questions that never were answered, the American public mourned the death of the warmhearted man, perhaps sensing that "normalcy" was a thing of the past—lost forever, like their president. History has since proven this through the wars, instability, and further eerie installments in *The Presidential Zero-Year Mystery*.

I am not sure that there is very much satisfaction about the President at any time. Of course, if one is a glutton for trouble he ought to be delighted with the office. Curiously enough, most of the men whom I know, who have been seekers after the

Presidency are those who care the least about encountering trouble, and if any of them ever comes to realize his ambition he will experience a rude awakening. (Warren G. Harding [July 13, 1922])

That is the way things go. If a man in politics complains about the way the winds blow he had better stay out of politics and out of the wind. (Harry Daugherty)

Franklin Delano Roosevelt— A Suspicious Affair

One thing is sure. We have to do something. We have to do the best we know how at the moment. If it doesn't turn out right, we can modify it as we go along. (President Franklin Delano Roosevelt [1933])

Look at the means which a man employs; consider his motives; observe his pleasures. A man simply cannot conceal himself. (Ancient Saying)

The enigmatic mystery of Franklin Roosevelt continues even now—almost four decades after his death. He was born into considerable wealth on January 30, 1882, at Hyde Park, New York. His admired fifth cousin, Theodore, had been born to wealthy parents, too. Yet as president, FDR spoke out with unclothed contempt

115

for "the economic royalists" and "the money-changers" that he would "drive from the temple" (much like Teddy's diatribes against the "vested interests" and "malefactors of great wealth"). Among other parallels (initial political careers in the New York legislature, both held the position of Assistant Secretary of the Navy, both became governors of New York, both were nominated as vice-presidential candidates, both were leaders of social revolutions), the most striking is that both became President of the United States, both publicly vowed they would refuse a third term, and both broke their promises.

To most of the general electorate, he was the "great hope" who led the country out of the worst depression in history, and led the country through one of the bloodiest wars known to mankind. To most he was the ultimate overcomer (as seen in his personal battle with infantile paralysis) and family man (his wife, Eleanor, and their six children all pursued successful life styles). Yet there remains another side to this so-called savior, especially concerning the "insiders" who supposedly "owned" him, the actions he allegedly took to unlawfully steer America into the catastrophic war (and the subsequent concessions at Yalta), the titillating stories of his extramarital affairs, and—in the end—the final hours of undisclosed activities preceding his death.

As in all cases of disputed greatness or weakness of America's presidents, even the historians widely disagree. The main difference between Roosevelt and Abraham Lincoln, for example, is the degree of disagreement. The Pulitzer Prize-winning historian Arthur M. Schlesinger, Jr., ranked FDR as one of the three top Chief Executives in America's history; the equally noted historians Dr. Harry Barnes and Charles Beard disclaimed much of Schlesinger's plaudits and proclaimed Roosevelt as a monumental charlatan. It is hard to retrace the past of such a man—savior to some, antichrist to others—but such an insight is needed to understand the increasingly eerie presidential death cycle.

Franklin's gracious Hudson River birthplace (an estate to most, a farm to FDR) served as his "home base" most of his life. As a boy he enjoyed private tutoring, touring abroad (he visited Europe eight times before he was sixteen), and feeling the attention that an only child of such an auspicious family could understand. He had his own pony at four and his own sailboat at sixteen. His father ("Popsie" to Franklin) was fifty-four when his son was born, but despite the age difference they seemed to relate well to each other, riding horses, hunting, sailing boats, swimming. From the beginning, Franklin was used to being the center of attention; "Popsie" and "Sallie" (his mother's real name was Sara Delano) gave him that attention, and though later FDR would naturally assume he would always get his own way (with his wife, children, and nation), the attention sometimes came in bittersweet ways.

When he was fourteen, the young prince was introduced to the sometimes less-than-friendly young people at Groton School in Massachusetts (most of the students were from families in the Social Register). His one great disappointment was reported to be his inability to win a letter on the school football team.

At the turn of the century, Roosevelt entered Harvard and enjoyed more success than at Groton. His famous cousin became president after McKinley's death, so Franklin's social prowess took notable upward momentum. He joined the prestigious Fly Club, and in his junior year he was elected editor of the Harvard *Crimson* (his ringing editorials cheered the football teams and expressed chagrin at "declining school spirit"). He maintained a C average at Harvard, graduating in 1904. In 1905 he married Eleanor Roosevelt (a distant cousin. The orphaned Eleanor was given away in marriage by her uncle, President Theodore, who remarked "It's a good thing to keep the name in the family."). After graduation from Harvard, and during the first two years of his marriage, Franklin attended Columbia Law School. He was bored by the studies and flunked several courses before dropping out altogether; still, he passed the bar examination anyway and took his place in a fashionable New York law firm.

Problems within his marriage reportedly surfaced soon after the wedding. Roosevelt had not shown much interest in young women until his junior year at Harvard. His first infatuation was directed toward Eleanor, a shy, plain, insecure orphan. Little is known of those first romantic encounters (later Eleanor destroyed his early letters to her), but she must have been impressed with his handsomeness (over six feet tall and slender), and he could have been attracted to her social concern (or her close connection to Teddy). Regardless, the two seemed incompatible from the beginning.

He was fun-loving; she was serious and cause-oriented. She was the product of an unhappy childhood; FDR could do nothing wrong in his parents' sight (his mother was unwilling to give up her only child during college—she moved to Boston to be close to Harvard, and in spite of his marriage to Eleanor, she insisted on setting up house with the young couple, dominated the house, and made all the crucial decisions. More than once, Sara Delano Roosevelt used "the allowance" as a viable weapon).

Family papers, made public for the first time in 1971, compared another striking contrast: Eleanor considered sex a necessary evil, while FDR had an unusually vigorous sexual appetite that would both create problems and tales during the years in Washington. After the sixth child was born in 1916, Eleanor refused his amorous advances permanently, and during the remaining twenty-nine years of marriage, she never slept with her husband again (in the White House, they actually occupied different sections).

The stage was set early in the marriage. The two went their separate ways, staying "married" partially for "Sallie" (remember the allowance?), and for public appearances. That the incompatibilities remained secret for so long points to either a terrific amount of information "locked" by the media from the public eye or to an inordinate web of concealment kept from the media.

Despite marital problems, Franklin "attracted" the attention of several Democratic "leaders" who were looking for a state senate candidate. He won an upset victory, and not only began a career in Albany, but supported Woodrow Wilson's 1912 presidential bid (Wilson had attacked "big business" while being supported by J.P. Morgan, the Rockefellers, and other international financiers. Wilson later "came through" by giving ultimate money control to these financiers through the highly secretive, uncontrolled Federal Reserve Board).

For his part in Wilson's 1912 campaign,

FDR was awarded an appointment as Assistant Secretary of the Navy, the same position Teddy had made famous fifteen years before. He served in this capacity from 1913 until 1920, proving himself a skillful and aggressive administrator.

The first marital upheaval came during this appointment. According to a book first published in 1946, Olive Clapper's *Washington Tapestry* (other books, some by the Roosevelt children, echoed the same basic story), Eleanor chanced upon a love letter that apparently revealed FDR's love and sexual relationship with Lucy Mercer. Eleanor proceeded to call her husband and the "other woman" to a conference, civilly offering a divorce and her blessings. Reportedly, Roosevelt's mother—not wanting her boy's reputation ruined—squelched all plans and no doubt reminded what she expected of everyone should Franklin want to continue receiving his generous allotment. It was all handled quietly, of course: "Sallie" won; Franklin and Eleanor went back to their working relationship; and Lucy had to keep a discreet distance, though the relationship would continue off and on until perhaps an hour or so before his death.

In 1920, Franklin became the vice-presidential candidate (with James M. Cox), but the Democratic hopefuls were soundly trounced by the Harding Administration. Shortly thereafter, Franklin entered the darkest period of his life.

In August, 1921, the thirty-nine-year-old was a picture of vibrant health. One evening at Campobello, New Brunswick, after a day of exercise and a swim in the icy Bay of Fundy, Roosevelt went to bed with a chill. The next morning he had a high temperature that was accompanied by acute pain in his legs. Within a few days his legs were paralyzed completely. Within a week the doctor diagnosed it as poliomyelitis.

The next few years were filled with tireless exercises and many trips to Warm Springs, Georgia, for water therapy. The president's grit surfaced during these years, an overcoming attitude that surprised many. In a strange way, his experience with polio only heightened his sense of personal infallibility. "If you have spent two years in bed trying to wiggle your big toe, then anything else seems easy," he once acknowledged.

Eventually, as he remained unshakably

resolved not to spend his life as an invalid, his condition did improve (through his hard work) enough so that he was able to "walk" using a cane, leg braces, and someone's supporting arm. "Walking" was an especially thrilling triumph since it allowed him to resume his political career.

At the 1924 Democratic Convention, he took the necessary steps from his chair to the platform, locked his braces, held the podium for support, and delivered a stirring, dramatic speech to nominate "the happy warrior," Alfred E. Smith. For Smith, it was the beginning of an unfortunate campaign, but for Roosevelt, it was an electrifying moment that would make the Democrats long remember his baritone voice and rousing manner.

During this same time, there were repeated whispers about Miss Marguerite (Missy) LeHand, Franklin's private secretary since the early 1920s. Roosevelt's paralysis probably strengthened his bond with Eleanor, but their relationship was one of mutual respect and dependence (for the family's sake) rather than personal love. At first it seemed impossible (even cruel) to believe the gossip, but medical reports proved FDR's sexual abilities remained unimpaired by the polio. Several decades later the Roosevelt's son, Elliott, published a book (*The Untold Story: The Roosevelts of Hyde Park*), in which he declared that Miss LeHand, FDR's tall, gray-eyed, prematurely gray-haired secretary, was Roosevelt's mistress for twenty years. Elliott further asserted that Eleanor not only knew about the relationship, but actually approved of it—even allowing Missy and Franklin to occupy adjoining bedrooms.

But the whispers were kept deliberately quiet. For one thing, the era of the twenties was filled with jazz, zany dancing, radio, Dillinger, and speak-easies. Who cared about old-fashioned morals? Those who did care did not know about Franklin and Missy. The plans for Roosevelt had to be kept rather whitewashed to be effective during the coming years.

In actuality, polio only served to increase FDR's appeal. In 1928, when Al Smith finally won the Democratic nomination for president, Roosevelt was persuaded to run for governor of New York to help lend strength to the ticket. Though Smith lost to Hoover, Roosevelt won by a narrow margin, used his office to advocate social reform for the needy (a timely subject as the winds of a coming depression increased), won a landslide reelection in 1930, and was the nearly unanimous Democratic nominee for president in 1932.

No doubt, a few Christians wondered if there was any numerologic significance in the 666 votes he received in garnering the nomination at the 1932 Chicago Democratic Convention. They had little time to wonder about numbers. The "Hoover Depression" had made *any* Democratic candidate a shoo-in. The 472 to 59 landslide hardly surprised anyone.

The prelude to President Roosevelt's first-term election was scarcely anything but an accident. There is much evidence that the Crash of 1929 had been scientifically engineered. The House Hearings on Stabilization of the Purchasing Power of the Dollar disclosed evidence in 1928 that the Federal Reserve Board (nonelected members of this board are appointed without fanfare or questioning for fourteen-year terms—and since its inception during Woodrow Wilson's administration the Federal Reserve Board is essentially a central money bank, without controls, with the power to control the money supply and interest rates and to manipulate the entire American economy) was working closely with the heads of European central banks. The committee further warned that the international financiers (and naturally the Federal Reserve Board who had been hand-picked by the financiers) were "tightening the noose." Shortly after Montagu Norman, governor of the Bank of England, came to Washington on February 6, 1929, to confer with Andrew Mellon, secretary of the treasury, the Federal Reserve Board immediately reversed the "easy-money" policy and began raising the finance interest rate. Then on October 24, 1929, the financiers (who had already quietly gotten rid of stock holdings) called back many key loans. Stockbrokers and customers who owed money to the financiers then had to dump stock on the market to pay the loans. This collapsed the stock market, began a banking collapse (bank runs created a panic, exhausted currency supplies, and caused closings). The investing public (who unfortunately did not know the crash was coming) took a collectively devastating blow. Millions were left jobless. But the "insiders" who engineered the crash later bought back the worthless stock at nearly a 100 percent discount from former highs.

After the election of November, 1932, President Hoover pleaded with Roosevelt to assure the country that he intended to abide by his conservative campaign promises. His silence, and whispered warnings that his administration was largely socialistic, caused rumors to spread that despite the promises, the country was heading for alarming monetary, economic, and social experiments.

The *New York Times* (June 16, 1934) and Wilbur and Hyde (in the book *The Hoover Policies*) both verified that the economic recovery which was well underway during Hoover's final year in office was deliberately sabotaged. In fact, unemployment during the Hoover Administration averaged just over six million annually. In the first two administrations of Franklin Roosevelt, by contrast, in spite of billions of dollars in appropriations for relief, annual employment was nearly ten million.

Eugene Lyons, the senior editor of *The Reader's Digest* for many years, and author of the book *The Herbert Hoover Story*, quoted Charles Michelson, chief of the Democratic Party publicity staff (during Roosevelt's 1932 campaign) as follows:

'The President-elect [FDR] told me on one occasion that the bank crisis was due to culminate just about inauguration day. . . . Naturally he did not care to have the dramatic effect of his intended proposals spoiled by a premature discussion of them in advance of their delivery.

So it is not surprising that within 100 days after his inauguration, Franklin Roosevelt and a willing press built his image around the concept of a dedicated, hardworking savior. Promising "action and action now," the fifty-one-year-old Roosevelt rushed through a series of measures with dazzling speed: the bank holiday, repeal of prohibition, vast appropriations to be used for relief, and help for the unemployed, homeowners, and farmers to be saved from foreclosure. Roosevelt's heavily Democratic Congress, also facing the crisis of the Depression, gave the president nearly everything he asked for. In rapid succession, they approved the National Recovery Act, the Agricultural Adjustment Act (drafted by Alger Hiss, one of Roosevelt's hand-picked insiders, later a self-admitted enemy of American free enterprise), and the Bituminous Coal Act, giving the growing federal bureaucracy unprecedented power.

Checks and balances placed in the Constitution to prevent such centralization of power worked for a time, especially since the Supreme Court declared early New Deal measures unconstitutional (the catchy phrase "New Deal" was supposed to have come from Mark Twain's *A Connecticut Yankee in King Arthur's Court*, but later evidence pointed to Roosevelt's having garnered the phrase from Stuart Chase's 1931-published book, *The New Deal*, in which Chase advocated socialistic ideals of the "successful" Soviet revolution and disparaged free enterprise. This same Stuart Chase was named in 1932 by Roosevelt to the National Resources Commission, and thereafter he climbed upward in the New Deal hierarchy, and finally settled in UNESCO, a United Nations agency, where he continued "reeducating" the world with the ideals of revolutionistic socialism).

The Supreme Court found many aspects of the New Deal to be in violation of the Constitution, and Roosevelt, infuriated, retaliated with schemes to bypass or replace the "nine old men." Even the New Deal-controlled Congress rejected his ill-fated "court-packing" plan, which would have allowed him to appoint new justices and remake the Supreme Court according to his wishes, a move which hardly seemed compatible with constitutional processes. Unfortunately, within two years of the "court-packing" scheme, the undaunted Roosevelt, through deaths and retirements, was able to control the court through his new appointments of four men: Hugo Black, Felix Frankfurter, Stanley Reed, and William O. Douglas. Surprisingly, none of the hand-picked four had any judicial experience prior to being named to the highest court in the land (this information is found in Gordon's book, *Nine Men Against America*).

With the carefully commandeered crisis, Franklin Roosevelt used every means available to assert his authority. Whether he did it for himself, for the best of the country, or as a puppet of "insiders" is all speculation. He did feel confident he would be able to bring America through one of its worst disasters. He did restore the confidence of the American populace at a time when that confidence was failing.

With unfailing courage born of his struggle against polio, he attacked what he called "the money-changers" (in spite of his own administration and his flock of advisors who had been hand-picked by the super rich). With a free-wheeling approach to America's deep problems, Roosevelt's New Deal programs provided some jobs and relief for the people, but it is safe to say that bureaucratic nightmares that have grown from such much-applauded developments as the Tennessee Valley Authority, the Social Security Act, and the Works Progress Administration have made his New Deal programs momentary panaceas rather than lasting benefits.

In fact, Roosevelt's enemies and friends alike began denouncing the "cures" as socialistic and threatening—even during the president's first term. Roosevelt's old friend Al Smith spoke of the dangers that would long outlast the temporary New Deal remedies.

But the press had promoted Roosevelt well. The populace remembered the panic and hunger of the Crash of 1929, and to them Roosevelt represented "economic security." Whatever it took to maintain that security was acceptable to them.

During the 1936 election, Alf Landon, "the Kansas sunflower," once again tried to warn the nation of the "cure-all" deals being made behind the scenes, but on November 3, 1936, the powerful Roosevelt/Garner team won one of the greatest landslides in American history (523 to 8 in the electoral college). If anything, the election was a tribute to the power of advertising (it has been no coincidence that a few "insiders" control the media mainstreams, by money and whatever else might be needed). The 1936 election also proved once again that the super rich could depend on the psychology of empty stomachs, knowing the masses would agree to anything rather than nothing—even if the present escape from miseries would later produce worse miseries.

Though the thirties had been mixed with dramatic but inefficient New Deal programs, only during the beginning of wartime productions did some level of prosperity return to the nation as a whole. As the ill winds drifted from the European and Asian conflicts during the late thirties, America and Roosevelt advocated an isolationist policy. If Roosevelt was aware of the Fascist menace on both sides of the oceans, he did not take the necessary steps to prepare the United States for war. He did provide crucial aid to Britain in the lonely fight against the Germans during 1940 and 1941, but there is much evidence that reflects his knowledge that the super rich were providing weapons and financing to *all* sides of the conflict, and some of Roosevelt's decisions seem to be based (in retrospect) upon the super rich rather than the good of his nation.

The campaign for Roosevelt's unprecedented third term proved to be another triumph for the ever-overcoming president. For months, he declined comment about running for a third term, neither saying he would (as many believed) nor refusing to run (as many wanted). His hesitation seemed to prevent any other Democrat from putting together a campaign against him. When he finally announced he would accept a "draft" in the Democratic Convention, the party had little choice but to draft him (who would change horses with the unceasing rumors of war?). One stunning move came when Roosevelt replaced Vice President Garner with then Secretary of Agriculture Henry Wallace. The party members were shocked at such a radical choice, especially with Wallace's alleged ties to known anti-Americans. It seemed to be an ill-fated choice until Eleanor Roosevelt made a forceful speech in behalf of her husand's choice at the convention. Together the Roosevelt/Wallace team won handily over Republican Wendell Wilkie, allowing Roosevelt to become the 1940 zero-year president.

Rumors of the "zero factor" once again surfaced. Had Wilkie been elected, it seems he would have been as doomed as the previous five zero-year presidents—he suffered a fatal heart attack on October 8, 1944.

Regardless, President Roosevelt once again resumed his office, though his popularity had slipped somewhat. There were numerous tensions—both on the surface and in secret. For one, his mistress, Missy LeHand, suffered a stroke in June, 1941, and died the next year. By that time, the Washington gossip mills were linking him with Crown Princess Martha of Norway, who in fact did spend most of the war years in the United States at the Pook's Hill, Maryland, estate that FDR had reportedly selected for her personally.

Whether the rumors were true is only partially substantiated, but it is known that during the latter years of the war, the president had once again rekindled the relationship with Lucy Mercer Rutherfurd, now a fifty-plus-year-old widow. For the remainder of his life, according to inside sources, he spent as much time with Lucy as possible.

It must be said that as Commander-in-Chief, he delegated authority to an unusually gifted group of men and backed them. Yet some of his actions still beleaguer historians. During 1941, Americans gave the Soviets, in knowing defiance of congressional laws prohibiting nonmilitary aid, billions of dollars of stockpiled nonmilitary supplies and materials. This became the foundation upon which the postwar Communist industrial machine was built (this information comes from Skousen's *The Naked Communist*). In 1943, unknown to Congress until later investigations, even before the United States had assembled its own atomic bomb, half of all American uranium and the technical information needed to construct an atomic bomb were sent to Russia (this information can be found in materials relating to the eighty-first congressional hearings). Also during the war, Roosevelt's assistant secretary of the treasury, Harry Dexter White (later reported to be an acknowledged anticonstitutional revolutionary), sent the Soviet Union engraving plates, paper, and ink to print "occupation currency" that would be totally redeemable by the United States Treasury (This information comes from the 1947 Armed Services and Banking Committee hearings). Political expediency may also have been behind Roosevelt's agreement with Joseph Stalin's demands for a "cross-channel" invasion of Europe (at the November, 1943, Cairo and Tehran conferences), despite Winston Churchill's angered objections and repeated urgings to attack Europe's soft "underbelly" (through Yugoslavia), which would have not only defeated Hitler, but also would have prevented the ultimate communist occupation of eastern Europe (this information can be found in 1947 Department of State papers).

At home, FDR approved the unconstitutional imprisonment of more than 100,000 Japanese-Americans in "relocation camps," yet abroad, he did nothing to rescue the doomed Jews of Europe, even after he learned that millions of them were being slaughtered in the Nazi holocaust.

But despite his critics, he was seeing Americans nearing victory as he ran for his fourth term. There were whisperings about his failing health, yet his renomination by the party seemed to be a foregone conclusion. The main problem was the continued public criticism of Vice President Henry Wallace. To avoid a convention floor fight (at least this was the official story), a little-known senator from Missouri named Harry S. Truman was selected to be Roosevelt's running mate. The Republicans, with New York Governor Thomas E. Dewey as the candidate, charged (with many examples—most notably the people connected with Roosevelt's administration and the forces behind the formulation of the United Nations) that anti-Americans were running the government, but they were unable to shake Roosevelt's image as an international war leader. Dewey lost; the vote was 432 to 99 in the electoral college.

His actions from January 20, 1945 (the inauguration when he appeared bareheaded and without an overcoat—despite the thirty-three-degree temperature—to give his fourth term address), to the Yalta Conference two weeks after the speech—all pointed to a particularly tormenting time of weakness and illness. At the Yalta meeting with

Churchill and Stalin, Roosevelt looked haggard and sickly and made some rather unusual concessions. His mind wandered, or so it was reported by informed sources. He was accompanied by his "advisor" Alger Hiss, who helped negotiate the pact that eventually gave Stalin and the Soviets the "freedom" to enslave 800 million Europeans and Chinese. In return for Stalin's promise to fight Japan (the Soviets were at war with Japan for an incredible six days), "Uncle Joe" (as Roosevelt called the dictator) was granted extraordinary rights in Asia and Eastern Europe (even though the Russians were scarcely needed, since Roosevelt already knew the atomic bomb would be used to end the war). Later, predictably, Stalin violated every Yalta agreement which guaranteed free elections in Europe. The secret agreements reached by the leaders caused many people in the free world to wonder if the thousands of soldiers and the tremendous expense of the war had been worth it. Obviously there was more to the picture than just Stalin's bargaining power.

With his doctor, Roosevelt conspired to keep his failing health a secret from the American public, so even Vice President

Truman was ill-prepared for the enormous responsibilities of the wartime presidency when the end came. But the end did come.

Little is known about the president's death. It is known that the president had gone to Warm Springs to rest and to prepare for the upcoming organizational meeting of the United Nations (which many of his hand-picked administrators and advisors had worked toward, and which the "super rich" had supported). One story related that he was posing for a portrait when he developed a headache, then slumped unconscious in his chair, only to die three hours later of a cerebral hemorrhage. His private secretary, Grace Tully, told a somewhat different version in her book that was published in 1949, *FDR—My Boss*. She reported that Lucy Mercer Rutherfurd had been with her longtime lover when he suffered the stroke. In the glut of books that have been written since then, other stories have surfaced. Some inside sources pointed to the president's total depression and possible suicide. Still others have even suggested that the four-term president was no longer useful to the "insiders" who had placed him in power.

Whatever the case, it appears that the truth was kept from the public. Eleanor Roosevelt refused to allow the casket to be opened for anyone, not even her sons. This peculiar act (and others) caused even greater suspicions.

Even after the mourning and eventual burial of the fallen leader (a plain white marble tombstone marks the Hyde Park grave of the thirty-second president), seamy and sordid details surfaced. But historians can only speculate. Historians can only uncover biased reports.

Was Roosevelt a truly great leader who served his country well and gave them confidence to overcome as he had overcome? Or was he, as one "insider" allegedly reported to Dr. William Wirt (as mentioned in a congressional investigation), a set-up puppet?

Wirt reported hearing the following description of Roosevelt:

> We are on the inside, we control the avenues of influence. We can make the President believe he is making the decisions for himself. Soon he will feel a superhuman flow of power from the flow of decisions themselves, good or bad.

Whether he was a "set-up" or not seems

immaterial now, especially since he was replaced by an even more enigmatic leader. For those looking for a "conspiracy behind every bush," there was much cause for alarm as the twelve years and thirty-nine days of Roosevelt's presidency definitely strengthened the power of the Chief Executive, weakened all other powers, and helped form the front group for a cacophony of anti-American forces.

But he was also the man who helped inspire men to reach beyond themselves as they pulled themselves out of postdepression pits and as they rallied together to stop the Axis powers.

Exactly why he did what he did will probably never be known. The sixth zero-year president in succession died with many of the answers locked inside. His life, career, motivations, friends, lovers, passions, and death—all are part of *The Presidential Zero-Year Mystery.*

8

John Fitzgerald Kennedy— Curious Camelot

We stand today on the edge of a new frontier—the frontier of the 1960s. Beyond that frontier are unchartered areas of science and space, unsolved problems of peace and war, unconquered pockets of ignorance and prejudice, unanswered questions of poverty and surplus.

It would be easier to shrink back from that frontier, to look to the safe mediocrity of the past. But I believe the times demand invention, innovation, imagination, decision. I am asking you to be new pioneers on that new frontier. (Sen. John F. Kennedy, presidential nomination acceptance speech, Los Angeles Democratic Convention, 1960)

Now I think that I should have known that he was magic all along. I did know

*it—but I should have guessed that it
would be too much to ask to grow old
with him and see our children grow up
together. So now he is a legend when he
would have preferred to be a man.*
(Jacqueline Kennedy, 1964)

The 1960 zero-year president was the
first of many things. He was the first president who had been born after the turn of
the century. He was the president during
the first major space explorations. He was
the first Roman Catholic to be elected to
the nation's highest office. He was the
youngest man ever to become the Chief
Executive, and as such he exhibited youthful drives and ambitions, and he developed
a rapport with a generation that had discovered Elvis Presley, drag racing, and
sock hops. America fell in love with his
wife, Jackie, and his little daughter, Caro-
line. We prayed and cried and waited—
then we learned that newborn Patrick had
died. We rejoiced when John-John learned
how to walk and imagined the Kennedys to
be the perfect family—especially when we
heard stories of the tousle-haired president allowing them to romp through the

oval office, and we saw pictures of the family touring toy stores.

He was Camelot—youth, strength, vigor. Then at 12:30 P.M., on November 22, 1963, America was interrupted by the bulletins on televisions and transistor radios. We died a thousand deaths as the assassination story unraveled. The television cameras were there in Washington to relay the funeral procession; again and again we saw the tragic moments in Dallas recounted, the empty horse, the stalwart Jacqueline. Camelot was gone.

Then Americans heard the Warren Report, and two-thirds of the people did not believe it. We learned that the man all America hated, Lee Harvey Oswald, may not have been the assassin. Or perhaps he was, but had he acted alone?

Then we heard verified reports that our fallen leader had been a womanizer, perhaps even while he was in the White House. We discovered his father had used his millions to "buy" into politics, and that "ol' Joe" had been rewarded for his "efforts" by being named U.S. ambassador to England during the Roosevelt Administration (by the super-rich money/politics manipulators). Then we heard more about Jack—

things we did not want to hear.

We were shocked, and hurt, and wondered how we could have been so naive. Camelot was indeed lost and gone forever. America was now plunged into the Johnson years of Vietnam, riots, and chaos.

What factors were behind the death of this warm, mystery-ridden, and energetic man who became the seventh successive zero-year president to die in office?

John Fitzgerald Kennedy was born in Brookline, Massachusetts, on May 29, 1917. On both sides, his grandfathers had been elite Irish political bosses. Joseph P. Kennedy, John's father, decided to seek power in another more lucrative way. He was a brilliant, manipulative money man, and by age twenty-five he had gained control of a Boston bank. He used his holdings and subsequent real estate investments to increase his profits through canny stock market purchases. He also invested in the lucrative liquor trade. Having succeeded on the East Coast (and after marrying Rose—the daughter of John "Honey Fitz" Fitzgerald), Joe Kennedy expanded to the West Coast and quickly garnered a fortune in the 1920s as a hard-driving film magnate and a ruthless stock operator who merged RKO and Pathe studios. Known as "the financial wizard of Hollywood," Joe became the center of attention of many famous and not-so-famous actresses (the latest exposé of his hobby of womanizing is found in Gloria Swanson's *Swanson on Swanson*). Within a few years, Joe Kennedy had built a financial empire worth a reported quarter of a billion dollars. For the remainder of his life (he died at age eighty-one in 1969), he used the clout of his empire to build a political reputation for his family.

From the beginning he sent his children to the best schools. Jack, the second oldest, attended prep school at Choate School (Connecticut). At Choate, he was known for both his lack of concern (he graduated in the bottom half of his class) and for his popularity (he was picked "most likely to succeed").

Life had been a constant confrontation between Jack and his brilliantly successful brother, Joseph Kennedy, Jr., so Jack chose Princeton University to further his education rather than the family-picked Harvard, where Joe was attending. After a bout with jaundice during the first year at Princeton, however, Jack dropped out of school and finally submitted to his parents' desire for him to attend Harvard.

Kennedy continued his unstudious ways (maintaining a C average) at Harvard, concentrating on football (until a back injury cut his career short) and avoiding confrontations with Joe, Jr. (it is said that Joe was often cruel in moving in on Jack's dates and friends, but by this time Jack was a slender six feet one, so he had no trouble acquiring new dates and new friends).

Since his father had begun serving as U.S. ambassador to England (a reward for his generous support of FDR), Jack temporarily dropped out of college during his junior year to travel abroad. During his period of voluntary research, he began preparing a study of England's complacency during the pre-World War II years. When he returned to Harvard, that thesis won a magna cum laude award and later became the best-selling book *Why England Slept.*

After a brief stint in Stanford's graduate school (after his graduation from Harvard), Jack accepted a commission as a navy officer, and within two years he became a decorated hero for his notable, life-saving exploits as the commander of a Pt boat that had been rammed and sunk by a Japanese destroyer.

While in the naval hospital back in the States, Jack learned that his older brother had been killed in a flying mission over Europe. The family was stricken by the tragedy, little knowing that the next decades would bring an uncanny string of tragedies.

After the war Jack decided on a writing career, but soon found that all the political aspirations once pinned on Joe Jr., were now resting on his young shoulders. In short order during 1946, the famous "Kennedy blitz" (family members campaigning everywhere) hit the Cambridge district with a well-organized emphasis on young Jack's war missions. Kennedy (and the Kennedys) won an easy victory.

The twenty-nine-year-old kid entered Congress in 1947, and the general impression among his colleagues was that he spent more time in Palm Beach than on Capitol Hill. This didn't seem to bother the Massachusetts voters, who twice reelected him by wide margins. During his six years in the House, newspapers and magazines frequently referred to him as one of the nation's richest, most eligible bachelors, and they made much of his attraction to pretty women and actresses (he was called "a chip off the old block"). Insinuations that he was a playboy before and after marriage did little to intimidate the Senator.

In 1952, the congressman and his family felt ready to challenge Henry Cabot Lodge, the incumbent Republican senator. Once again the "Kennedy blitz" hit, generously financed by daddy (the financing also included a "business loan" of a reported half million dollars to the *Boston Post*, a newspaper that came out soon after the "loan" heavily endorsing the Democratic candidate). In short order, the thirty-five-year-old candidate became both a United States senator *and* a new husband (he was married in 1953 to Jacqueline Bouvier, a twenty-three-year-old daughter of a socially climbing Wall Street stockbroker).

Though he was neither particularly impressive nor successful in the Senate chambers, his image inspired the people's confidence. His emergence on the national scene during 1956 in an ill-fated vice-presidential try coincided with a book he had reportedly written during his recuperation from back surgery. The book, a detailed description of past senators who had dared to vex public opinion, *Profiles in Courage*, became a best seller in 1956 and won the prestigious Pulitzer Prize in 1957. In actuality, however, the book was a collaborative effort by Ted Sorensen (Kennedy's legislative assistant) and Dr. Jules Davids (a history professor at Georgetown University). Kennedy, who mainly did a lot of overseeing and little actual writing (according to Herbert Parmet's *Jack: The Struggles of John F. Kennedy*), was given sole authorship of the book. Since Joseph, Sr., heavily promoted the book, it is not surprising it became such an acclaimed success. Because of the book, Kennedy's name was thereafter associated with "political courage," even though during his bedridden time (when he was overseeing the writing of the book), he was noticeably quiet (refusing to declare himself on the issue) during the Joseph McCarthy censure debates.

By 1960, Kennedy had emerged as a picture of health, a literary giant, and a leading candidate for the Democratic nomination (he had just swept the reelection campaign in a state-record landslide). Conjectures about his morals were expressed (there was a particularly spicy story about

Jackie's intents to leave the marriage, until she was persuaded to stay by Papa Joe), but the biggest concern was over his religion. No Roman Catholic had been elected before to the nation's highest office, but in the final analysis, Jack's personality and terrific speaking ability (especially prominent in the famous Kennedy/Nixon TV debates) gave him a slight edge. On November 8, 1960, John Fitzgerald Kennedy became the nation's thirty-fifth president by a margin of only 49.9 percent to Nixon's 49.6 percent of all the votes. There were comments even then that Nixon was "lucky" not to have been elected on the "cursed" zero year. In fact, while still a candidate, Kennedy had addressed the subject:

The historical curiosity is indeed thought-provoking: Since 1840 every man who has entered the White House in a year ending with a zero has not lived to leave the White House alive. . . . On face value, I daresay, should anyone take this phenomenon to heart—anyone, that is, who aspires to change his address to 1600 Pennsylvania Avenue—that most probably the landlord would be left with a "For Rent" sign hanging on the gate-house door. (From a letter, Library of Presidential Papers, New York)

The whispers continued for a time, but were forgotten, especially after the crowd-thrilling Inauguration Day (January 20, 1961), when the new president delivered the lines that would soon become his eulogy: "Ask not what your country can do for you, but what you can do for your country."

Jack and Jackie were the national sweethearts, dazzling the populace with youthful vigor and fashion. People were totally impressed by his sense of humor.

Soon, however, the cruel weight of the nation's highest office crushed down upon him. Campaign promises and smiles were soon replaced by cold realities.

As a candidate he had criticized Eisenhower's Cuban policy as being lenient:

> We must attempt to strengthen the non-Batista democratic anti-Castro forces in exile, and in Cuba itself, who offer eventual hope of overthrowing Castro. Thus far, these fighters for freedom have had virtually no support from our government. (Campaign speech, October 20, 1960)

After being promised governmental support, a fourteen-hundred-men force of anti-Castro Cubans invaded communist Cuba at Cochinos Bay (known as "The Bay of Pigs") on April 17, 1961, only three months after JFK's inauguration. It is common knowledge that the invasion was planned, financed, and controlled (with Kennedy's approval and promise of air cover) by the United States State Department and the Central Intelligence Agency.

As planned, the force reached the beaches and in a short time had dealt heavy blows to Castro's troops. The anti-Castro militants were confident, even as the communist tanks advanced, since the pre-invasion planning had included Kennedy's assurances of Cuban-piloted B-26s, a maneuver that would have destroyed most of the Soviet puppet's troops. But the planes never came; the use of the Cuban air force was forbidden at the last moment. As reports of the blood bath that resulted surfaced, other sordid details also were uncovered— deliberate sabotage of the underground uprisings that were to have taken place all over the island, spotty and inadequate communications from the Chief Executive to the leaders of the overthrow.

One year later, Kennedy was again faced with another crisis in Cuba, this time over Soviet missile sites. To some, JFK was a hero, the leader of America's greatest cold war victory. To others, he had overreacted initially, and once the saber rattling was over, he had apparently failed to see that missile silos continued to be built in Cuba.

Kennedy did champion a progressive and strong domestic program, but his handling of Congress was relatively unsuccessful (none of the major domestic proposals of his "New Frontier" programs were ever enacted). He was a leader in the civil rights movement, yet was often reluctant to make a commitment to his promises for equal rights.

What he might have been, or done, or finished—all is pure speculation. On November 22, 1963—President John F. Kennedy became the seventh Chief Executive to fall victim to the "zero factor." In moments, his life had been extinguished by bullet wounds in the neck and head. He was forty-six, had lived a shorter life than any other president, and was buried in Arlington National Cemetery beneath an "eternal flame" memorial.

But the controversy over his death has raged since. At first, the public was outraged at the poker-faced Lee Harvey Oswald. Then Americans were shocked at the "superpatriot" Jack Ruby, who in a flurry of televised activity, shot the alleged assassin. The Warren Commission searched through evidence and published the now-famous Warren Report, which two-thirds of the public refused to believe.

At first, Lee Harvey Oswald was an easy target for America's anger. He was a man who had turned his back on his country to live in Russia, then came back to America spouting pro-Castro ideologies. Even after the fatal shot was fired at him in the Dallas City Hall basement, Oswald was still guilty. Or so everyone thought.

Then an amazingly accurate tape evaluation of Oswald's statements by a near-precise scientific instrument, the Psychological Stress Evaluator (read George O'Tool's *The Assassination Tapes*) proved (at least to many investigators) that Lee Harvey Oswald was innocent in the assassination of John F. Kennedy.

As further evidence was uncovered and hushed (there were suspicious deaths of key witnesses), in 1967 New Orleans District Attorney Jim Garrison announced he had uncovered the assassination conspiracy (that most Americans believed existed) and had brought an indictment against Clay Shaw, a New Orleans businessman.

But two years later, after many sordid facts surfaced and a courtroom debacle cost Garrison his credibility, Shaw was released.

But instead of "putting the matter to rest," the new findings have merely continued to add public opinion to the disapproval of the alleged "cover-ups." Congressional members (George Murphy, Strom Thurmond, Russell Long, and many others), religious leaders (Bishop Fulton J. Sheen for one), and notable historians have agreed about the conspiracy theory. In other words, as some would purport, the conspiracy theories have not been limited only to a few muckraking journalists and public officials.

If a conspiracy did kill President Kennedy, how it was accomplished becomes extremely important. The purely mechanical aspect was brilliantly reconstructed by Josiah Thompson in *Six Seconds in Dallas*. The logistical and tactical elements investigated most thoroughly by District Attorney Jim Garrison add to the scientific analysis of how it happened. From all the information, a new picture has been conclusively drawn—the most startling point being that in all probability, the final and fatal shot was fired by a .45-caliber automatic from a sewer vent to the front and right of President Kennedy's motorcade.

Piecing the elements together, the most plausible evidence has led to a precision guerrilla team of at least seven men. Of the witnesses in Dealey Plaza, almost two-thirds said that the shots came from the grassy knoll area in front and to the right of the presidential limousine, not from the book depository (as the Warren Report asserted). Reliable eyewitnesses heard shots come from behind the picket fence (in front of the motorcade) and saw a puff of smoke in that area. In a film published by *Life* magazine (and among the other photo-documents, both professional and amateur), it is evident the president was slammed backward by the impact of a bullet, which means—with little doubt—that he was shot from the front. In fact, several of the doctors at Dallas's Parkland Hospital pointed to the neck wound being an entrance wound (not a shot fired from the back through the head). From sorting through the evidence and photographs, it is certain that there were at least two men behind the picket fence, four men on the grassy knoll, and at least two behind a small stone wall to the right of the fence. At least two other men fired from behind the President, one from the Texas Book Depository (not Oswald), and one from the Dal-Tex Building. There were suspects taken into custody from each of these areas, but later they dropped out of sight and have remained anonymous. In addition, another man, dressed in green combat fatigues, acted out a distracting, simulated epileptic seizure near the grassy knoll just before the president's motorcade had reached the fatal point.

From Flammonde's *The Kennedy Conspiracy*, this precise operation was exactly the plan that had been discussed and plotted during September, 1963, in David Ferrie's New Orleans apartment (several men, including Clay Shaw and Lee Harvey Oswald, were allegedly in the meeting). So from all angles, after piecing together the information (much concealed and overlooked by the "authorities"), it seems the assassination was a precise, coordinated operation. Lee Harvey Oswald was—in all probability—a "set-up" scapegoat.

Flammonde also pieces some amazing, after-the-fact elements together: Jack Ruby knew Lee Harvey Oswald (though everyone connected denied any association between the two, yet they were seen together on more than one occasion prior to the shooting, and Oswald's coded telephone book included Ruby's private telephone number); Jack Ruby was associated with Clay Shaw (a reported "queen-bee" of the New Orleans underworld who, according to Jim Garrison, masterminded the entire operation); Ruby knew David Ferrie (who reportedly also helped plan and implement the assassination plot and was linked in the conspiracy to Oswald and Shaw until his "suicide"); and finally, Jack Ruby (according to the Warren Report) repeatedly asked Justice Warren to allow him (Ruby) to be taken away from Texas to the safety of Washington to tell "why my act was committed, but it can't be said here," yet was refused by Warren even though he had been granted subpoena power to take Ruby to the nation's capital. But the tale of his "act" was never told. Ruby spoke about threats on his life in Dallas, and within months after the final talk with Warren, he was dead of cancer (Norman Mailer, among others, have charged that he was injected with live cancer cells to prevent his transfer from the control of certain

Dallas police).

Other *how* questions go unanswered. For example, even though the FBI had sent out TWXs (bureau telegrams) on November 17, 1963, announcing that an assassination attempt would be made on President Kennedy in Dallas on November 22, yet for some reason the president was allowed to ride in the parade without the prepared bubble-top (limousine canopy) and without the proper protection.

Even today the same questions keep arising—the latest is British author Michael Eddowe's crusade to have Lee Harvey Oswald exhumed, stating evidence that Oswald was really a Soviet "plant."

And if the questions of how it happened remain, then certainly the question of why it happened must be raised as well. People have pointed many fingers since November 22, 1963—some with much evidence to back their allegations.

A recent book, *Conspiracy*, by Anthony Summers, is one of the most unusual attempts to answer some of the *how* and *why* questions. He states that at least four, not three (as the Warren Commission reported), shots were fired in Dealey Plaza. This leads to three possible centers of conspiracy (any one of which could fit with the theories of Flammonde, Garrison, and others): a renegade element in the American intelligence community (perhaps bought or controlled by the "super rich"); or the Mafia (always somewhat an enemy of the "manipulators," plus JFK's attorney general—Robert Kennedy—had prosecuted the Mob more vigorously than any attorney general before or since); or anti-Castro Cubans (who felt betrayed by the Bay of Pigs incident). All three of these suspected groups had a common interest—Cuba. The intelligence agents were still intent on overthrowing Castro. The syndicate wanted to regain lucrative gambling and prostitution interests in Havana. And the anti-Castro Cubans were probably most interested in regaining their homeland.

No one will really ever know all the facts. There are so many questions that will probably never be answered—someone (or some people) have too much to lose.

The twisted, unexplained assassination has caused incredible stories (some based on facts, some on suppositions) concerning President Kennedy. A few years back, someone finally asked why no one had seen the body except for a few doctors after the president was taken into Parklane's Trauma One. That led to the recurring "empty coffin" theory (that has been whispered about other dead presidents)—that President Kennedy was still alive: some have "proven" he is a "vegetable" in a Denver facility, often visited by Jackie; and others have "proven" he is living somewhere in the South Pacific, far away from the enemies who tried to kill him. The same "empty coffin" theories have led to tales about Hitler and Elvis Presley, even people who swear that the "dead" people have been seen living in obscurity.

The sad facts point out that President Kennedy indeed died, and that in becoming the seventh consecutive zero-year president to fall victim to the death-cycle, he shared many similarities in death with the others—none more so than with President Lincoln.

Both Abraham Lincoln and John Fitzgerald Kennedy were elected in the sixtieth year, one century apart; both after famous debates (Lincoln with Douglas, Kennedy with Nixon); both on a strong civil rights platform. Both lost a child while president (Willie Lincoln and Patrick Kennedy).

Both were slain on a Friday in the presence of their wives. Both were advised not to go to their destinations where the assassinations happened (a secretary named Kennedy tried to get Lincoln not to go to the Ford Theater; a secretary named Lincoln tried to get Kennedy not to go to Dallas, but the president did anyway).

The men who were initially named assassins (though there were later questions surrounding possible accomplices) were both Southern radicals. Booth committed the crime in a theater and ran to a warehouse before being caught, while Oswald supposedly committed the crime in a warehouse and ran to a theater before being caught. Both Booth and Oswald were murdered before they faced trial; neither one was allowed to "tell his side of the story" of the conspiracy before impartial listeners.

Lincoln's successor, like Kennedy's, was named Johnson. Andrew Johnson was born in 1808; Lyndon Johnson was born in 1908—both were former senators, and both were Southern Democrats.

Does history repeat itself? Was it a mere coincidence? Why are there so many unanswered questions? What really destroyed Camelot?

As with each of the ill-fated Chief Executives, the wound from Dallas still aches—one more eerie, mocking monument in *The Presidential Zero-Year Mystery*.

9

Will History Repeat Itself?

*One sobering fact of history will over-
shadow the 1980 elections—the so-called
"20-year curse." Strange at it seems,
since 1841 every U.S. President elected
on a 20-year interval has died in office:
Kennedy in 1963, Roosevelt in 1945,
Harding in 1923, McKinley in 1901,
Garfield in 1881, Lincoln in 1865 and
William H. Harrison in 1841. Four
were assassinated, three died of heart
attack or disease.*

*In 1980, neither vice-presidential can-
didate should be chosen as a ticket-
balancing afterthought, for one of these
men may well serve as President.* (Pat
Robertson [quoted from *Perspective*, a
special report to members of the 700
Club])

The "sobering fact" and caution both

seemed to "overshadow the 1980 elections"—just as the great electronic evangelist had predicted. "Modern" Americans—like the rest of the world—live fatalistic and superstitious lives, perhaps not as much as past generations, but quite prone to give "luck" or "fortune" the blame or credit. Pat Robertson analyzed human nature well.

When a person rises from the back alleys of New York to celluloid stardom, it's because he has been "lucky" or "gotten the good breaks." When a man's hair begins to thin when he reaches thirty, he is consoled with the fact that his dad and grandfather also began losing their manly manes at thirty; to most, "one's lot in life" cannot be escaped. If heart attacks run traditionally in a family tree, for example, all the branches resign themselves to "meeting their fate" through a heart attack. "Fate is fixed," people sigh, "so why try to fight it?"

So when Pat Robertson wrote about the 1980 presidential election, he candidly shared what most Americans were already thinking: there is a strong possibility that history would once again be repeated, that the new President of the United States would become a victim of "zero factor." Regardless, even before the 1976 election was over, and long before the "mid-term" 1978 elections were held, America had candidates for the 1980 presidential nomination. Lots of them. Maybe over a hundred. America's quadrennial three-ring circus— the panic-stricken scrambling for votes and the attention of the media—got off to the earliest start ever. Commented Sen. Bob Dole of Kansas, one of the early Republican candidates: "I'm surprised nobody has started running for 1984 on the theory that you can't start too early any more."

Perhaps most to blame for the increasingly premature impetus was President Carter himself, especially since he had begun campaigning nearly three years in advance of the 1976 election—and made it work by coming out of relative obscurity in Georgia to win his party's nomination and the White House.

Success breeds success, so dark-horse and leading contenders alike joined the stampede that would hopefully lead to a November 4, 1980, ticket to the White House.

Incumbent President Jimmy Carter headed the list, and though he seemed to toy with the press at first, he was a definite candidate long before he officially declared. Of all the Democrat candidates, by early 1980, only Edward Kennedy and Jerry Brown seemed viable contenders. The Republican ticket was bloated with hopefuls: Ronald Reagan, John Connally, Howard Baker, George Bush, Bob Dole, Philip Crane (who established an early-bird record when he declared for the GOP presidential nomination on August 2, 1978), John Anderson, and Lowell Weicker (who dropped out of the race on May 16, 1979, even before most rivals had even announced).

And with the political pot boiling (much too early), the primary process to produce America's "finest" leadership had begun—nonstop months of living in motels, racing frantically from state to state, looking pleasant but ducking issues rather than pondering them, placing more emphasis on the twenty-second shot (a line written by an advertising agency speech writer) on the CBS "Evening News" than on the real problems affecting the citizenry, being pressured to wear a hard hat in Pittsburgh and a feathered headdress in New Mexico rather than facing the economic crunch with realistic measures.

During the 1980 struggles, show business people were produced to smile and wave at rallies across the nation: Paul Newman, Warren Beatty, Elizabeth Taylor, Bob Hope, Jane Fonda, Joan Baez, Linda Ronstadt, the Eagles, Robert Redford, Efrem Zimbalist, Jr., Marlon Brando, Donny and Marie Osmond, and many others.

And the growing born-again Christian movement began creating a forceful voice. This was especially obvious by mid-1980, because the Republican slot had been clinched by believer Ronald Reagan, the Democratic nomination (despite last-ditch attempts by Kennedy forces) was held by Jimmy Carter (a Baptist believer who helped popularize the term "born again" in 1976), and the leading independent candidate, John Anderson, an Evangelical Free church member also claimed to be born again. This emphasis on evangelical Christian beliefs had surfaced to cause both excitement and alarm. When 1980 Gallup Polls reflected a two-year rise in the number of born-again Christians from one-third of the populace to 53.4 percent, it did not take political analysts long to compute the possibilities.

Naturally, since the Church has historically shunned election fights, the new awareness and involvement of millions of born-again Christians caused many to raise voices of concern and caution. Television producer Norman Lear met with liberal Protestants at the National Council of Churches to discuss a possible series of advertisements warning against "the threat of religious demagoguery" in the campaign. Sen. George McGovern, his own campaign being threatened by the new force, blasted the "zealotry, self-righteousness and vindictiveness" of the born-again movement. Sen. Birch Bayh, also under fire from conservative Christians, accused the Christian right of "falsification and distortion." One of Reagan's aides said, "The marriage of religion and politics is the most dangerous thing, the creepiest thing I've ever seen" (*U.S. News and World Report*, September 15, 1980).

The rapid growth of the evangelistic broadcasting networks worried some (the "unofficial" word that came down to the evangelists from the governmental "powers that be" was to stay away from the subject of politics, or "problems" on the affiliate levels might result; needless to say, those bureaucratic warnings were largely ignored), but for the first time, as four million Christians registered to vote for the first time (according to Jerry Falwell), and as evangelists such as James Robison, Pat Robertson, and Jim Bakker urged Christian participation at all levels of government—all three major candidates and the media began to realize the importance of the born-again vote. Rev. Bob Maddox was chosen by President Carter to mend fences with the evangelicals, and Baptist minister Bob Billings was enlisted by the Reagan camp to woo support.

Grass-roots organizations were set up to encourage support and urge electronic church viewers to vote. During 1980, a number of stunning upsets were engineered by such groups as Falwell's Moral Majority and the controversial Christian Voice. Hundreds of conservative Christians played a major role in the formation of the Republican platform (Republican National Committee general counsel Ben Cotten said afterwards, "Anyone who doesn't think they had a big hand in reshaping our platform is kidding himself. When these people decide that something is important to their principles, it's 'Katy, bar the door.'").

But the door was opened—"It's time for God's people to come out of the closet and the churches—and change America," thundered Fort Worth evangelist James Robison, and millions of born-again Christians responded with decisive votes.

Three men (and their running mates) found themselves on the threshold of history—the 1980 zero-year election.

James Earl Carter, Jr., was born in Plains, Georgia, a small town in Sumter County, on October 1, 1924. His father was a grocery store manager and the owner of two other businesses. His mother, Lillian, was a nurse.

Southern politics, peanut farming, and the Baptist faith were three important elements to young Jimmy, his two sisters, and his brother. "We felt close to nature," he wrote later, "close to the members of our family, and close to God."

After Plains High School (he played basketball and dreamed of going to the United States Naval Academy), Jimmy Carter studied one year at Georgia Southwestern College in Americus, one year at Georgia Tech, then entered the U.S. Naval Academy as a plebe in 1943. He graduated in 1946 with honors, married his hometown sweetheart—Rosalynn Smith—shortly after finishing at the academy, and began seven years of assignments in the navy.

Jimmy's naval career was cut short by his father's death in 1953. He resigned his commission, returned to Plains, and began building a drought-ridden farming business into one of the most efficient and well-managed peanut wholesalers in Georgia.

From 1955 to 1962, he served on the Sumter County Board of Education, was active in civic affairs, and nurtured a growing desire to enter politics. Much of his time was also given to his growing family (Jack, Chip, Jeff, and Amy).

In 1962, Carter entered state politics, winning a disputed battle for the Georgia senate. After another term, he lost the 1966 election for governor of Georgia. He once again ran for governor in 1970 (gave 1,800 speeches) and won. While still serving as governor of Georgia, he began planning for a future career.

On December 12, 1974, Carter officially announced himself as a candidate for the nation's highest elected office, and for nearly two years he enacted the Georgia version of Kennedy's "Boston blitz"—all the family was involved in shaking hands, making speeches, and smiling nonstop smiles. He was an unknown but found himself backed by some of the nation's "insiders." He also attracted a growing percentage of Americans with the revelation of his born-again Christian beliefs. At the Democratic convention, he was nominated on the first ballot and chose Sen. Walter F. Mondale of Minnesota as his running mate.

In a "common man" campaign against Republican incumbent Gerald Ford, Carter emerged from peanut farmer to president. On November 2, 1976, the electorate gave him 50.1 percent of the vote. The electoral college made it official, 297 votes to Ford's 241.

During the next four years, campaign promises proved hard to fulfill, yet he did win approval of his economic stimulus program, raised the minimum wage and farm price supports, and received authority to remodel the federal bureaucracy. He actively facilitated the peace initiatives of President Anwar Sadat and Premier Menachem Begin.

Conservatives noted with alarm that Jimmy Carter was a member of the Trilateral Commission and the Council of Foreign Relations (both arms of the Rockefeller-led "super-rich" invisible government). Also of considerable interest to conservatives was the fact that the Trilateral Commission was the 1973 brainchild of Carter's National Security Adviser, Zbigniew Brzezinski, who in his 1970-published book, *Between Two Ages*, had praised Marxism, wrote about the obsoleteness of United States free enterprise, and proposed planning of United States national sovereignty into a community of nations—with an eventual goal of world government.

Craig Karpel wrote an article for *Penthouse* (November, 1977), in which he also shouted warnings for the nation:

> The Presidency of the United States and the key Cabinet departments of the federal government have been taken over by a private organization dedicated to the subordination of the domestic interests of the United States to the international interests of the multinational banks and corporations. This seizure of public power by private interests is the most serious political scandal in American history.

Somehow it still seems incongruous that the soft-spoken, deeply religious thirty-ninth president could also be David Rockefeller's protégé and be privy to "the unelected rulers" of world governments (more about that in chapter ten). Maybe the conservative press made too much ado about Carter's involvement with Rockefeller, but a Washington *Post* reporter (William Greider, June 22, 1978) revealed that at least eighteen top-level executives of the Carter Administration had been drawn from the Trilateral membership.

Could it all have been a mistake? Was the right-wing press trying to smear the born-again president because of his liberal views on abortion, ERA, and welfare? Somewhere the truth was woven among the multicolored fabric, and the nation seemed intent on seeing the real Jimmy Carter. Much of the nation saw him as a devoted leader and worked for his reelection. Others saw him as the antithesis of true American values. The battle lines were drawn ever tightly as November 4, 1980, approached. By midnight, the results were clear.

John Bayard Anderson turned out to be a surprise to many during the 1980 GOP primary races and his attempt to run for president on the Independent Party ticket (with former Wisconsin Governor Patrick Lucey as his running mate).

When it became evident that the Republican Party was going to nominate Ronald Reagan, Anderson remarked, "Republicans seem all too anxious to snatch defeat from the jaws of victory, and we'll do the same in 1980 if we nominate an ultraconservative."

Shortly afterward, he announced his continued try as an Independent. The lean, white-haired Illinois representative emerged, boldly endorsing social programs while urging a tight-fisted approach to government spending.

His attempt to become the fortieth president of the United States was an uphill battle, at best, but one-sided struggles had always been part of his long-term political career.

Anderson was born on February 15, 1922, in Rockford, Illinois; his father and mother operated a grocery store. His father had emigrated from Sweden not long before. The family was deeply religious; they were members of the First Evangelical Free Church of Rockford. One of John's childhood dreams was to become a minister, and though his career took a different direction, he has continued speaking at lay classes and conducting Bible studies. He, like the other two leading 1980 presidential candidates, openly talked of a strong belief in God:

> Religion is a great source of comfort because we don't have all the answers. We are limited in our finite ways to provide solutions. Having religious faith fills a tremendous vacuum.
> —*U.S. News and World Report* (November 26, 1979)

The studious Anderson developed his oratory and intellectual skills in high school (he was class valedictorian) and at the University of Illinois (he earned Phi Beta Kappa honors). His law studies at Illinois University were temporarily interrupted by action in World War II, but he resumed his schooling after the war, and in 1946 received his law degree.

In 1952, he received enough attention from influential people to be named an adviser to the United States Commissioner in West Germany (Keke Machakos was the photographer at the passport division of the State Department at that time; getting a passport photo taken led Anderson to a date with Keke, marriage in 1953, and five children).

After three years in Germany, John and

Keke Anderson returned to Illinois, intent on entering politics. He was elected the state's attorney in 1956. In 1960, he became a U.S. representative from Illinois. He soon became known for the blend of social liberalism and financial conservatism that was to later mark his presidential aspirations.

John Anderson had supported Richard Nixon's election in 1968, but became estranged from the White House during the Vietnam and Watergate controversies. In 1974, he was one of the influential members of Congress who encouraged Nixon to resign.

In 1978, he survived a serious fight in the Republican primary for his seat from northwest Illinois. By November of that year, he had not only been reelected, but was being mentioned as a GOP contender for the office of Chief Executive.

During 1980, as it became evident he could not win the nomination from Reagan, the Independent Party idea gained momentum. In modern times, third-party candidates had been successful only because of a regional appeal (Strom Thurmond in 1948 and George Wallace during the sixties and seventies).

From the beginning of the race, however, he was a dismal third. Undaunted, he continued. A crucial decision by the Federal Election Commission gave some hope for federal campaign subsidies after the election if he received at least 5 percent of the votes. He received endorsements from some liberal leaders. It was little surprise (especially since he is a member of Rockefeller's Trilateral Commission) that he received millions in loans from eastern banks to finance his campaign. And on September 21, 1980, he was viewed by a national television audience as he enthusiastically debated Ronald Reagan. His camp emphasized "The Anderson Difference" as they cited the sharp contrasts between the moderate Carter and conservative Reagan.

But realistically, John Anderson was primarily a romantic distraction for voters who were unhappy with both major party candidates. "Mr. Anderson," said President Carter during September, "is primarily a creation of the press."

Against all the temptations to retire on his Rancho del Cielo near Santa Barbara, California, *Ronald Wilson Reagan* allowed himself to be persuaded that it was his duty to once again attempt the agonizing climb to the presidency, an aspiration that had eluded him on previous tries.

Burning with a conviction that America was not dead—as some believed—but only suffocating under the bureaucratic weight of governmental red tape, former California Governor Reagan announced his candidacy for the GOP nomination early in the race, and within weeks he seemingly eclipsed all other Republican contenders. Only George Bush remained a distant second. But by convention time, it was evident that a conservative element was no longer the "sleeping giant" but had become a thunderous voice. The star-spangled convention hall in Detroit rang with unifying "Let's Make America Great Again" slogans.

After a brief hiatus, Reagan and his entourage hit the campaign trail again, this time intent on trading a dream for reality. That dream was the byproduct of sixtynine years of preparation.

Ronald Reagan was born the second son of Jack and Nelle Reagan in a small town— church-going, flag-waving Tampico, Illinois. He grew up hearing tales about the Illinois prairie, and he was a gradeschooler when the triumphant, battered

World War I doughboys returned to Main Street parades. America was the conqueror over every evil, and every red-blooded American boy dreamed of fighting for his country.

Ronald was a teen-ager in Dixon, Illinois, when he thrilled to the sight of Charles Lindbergh barnstorming overhead. He graduated from Dixon's North High ("Dutch" fell in love with sports) in 1928. Even though the Great Crash hit during his first year at Eureka College, Reagan continued his education, playing varsity football, swimming, and using his photographic memory rather than study skills to get through his academics. He was a clean-cut, Christian, all-around student—mainly remembered by his classmates for his wit, enthusiasm, and grit.

His nurtured love for acting and radio broadcasting led to his first job as a five-dollar-a-week sportscaster for WOC in Davenport, Iowa. Within a year he had graduated to a whopping seventy-five dollars a week at WHO in Des Moines, and for five years, until he turned twenty-six, he became *the* voice (known as "Dutch" Reagan) for the leading mid-America station. He became a local celebrity.

But he wanted more, so through some old WHO friends trying to find a break in Hollywood, he decided to move to California.

In short order, he was signed to Warner Brothers, and during the next thirty-three years, he became one of the best-known tinsel-town stars, married twice, served during World War II, caused some controversy as president of the Screen Actors Guild, and hosted two long-running television series.

As he became more politically minded during the late fifties and early sixties, some Republicans urged him to enter politics actively, but it was his 1964 appeal in behalf of Barry Goldwater that surprised much of the nation with Reagan's enthusiasm and speaking expertise.

By 1965, he was being openly courted to enter the California gubernatorial race. In a highly efficient campaign he destroyed incumbent Pat Brown. At the inaugural dinner in Sacramento, he was toasted as "the future President of the United States."

As a candidate to "cut and squeeze and trim" the state's burgeoning bureaucracy, Reagan entered the governor's mansion full of dreams. During the next two terms, those dreams were replaced by hard-fought realities. He didn't do all he had hoped to do (cutting the budget and cutting spending), but he left the state in better shape than it was in when he was first elected.

By 1968 he had developed a sense of responsibility to run for the presidency, but he waited too long to begin in earnest, and the GOP nominated Richard Nixon. Then in 1976, when it seemed he had an edge (largely on his conservative stances) on Gerald Ford, he made a tragic political blunder by picking Sen. Richard Schweiker (a Pennsylvania liberal) as his running mate. The choice disillusioned even many of his most staunch supporters and surprised some of his colleagues. But the decision had been made, and eventually Gerald Ford was picked to run against the Georgia dark horse.

Even though the Republican candidate would be facing an incumbent Democrat, 1980 proved to be Reagan's year. From the beginning, political analysts, feeling the conservative backlash so evident among the nation's people, focused attention on Ronald Reagan's popularity. By midsummer, the other Republican contenders were completely out of the picture.

The campaign against Jimmy Carter began in earnest long before the Republican convention was held. In a sense, the campaign featured an ultraconservative who had—for some unknown reason—picked a moderate (George Bush—a member of Rockefeller's Trilateral Commission along with Carter, Mondale, and Anderson), against a moderate Democratic candidate.

By October, *U.S. News and World Report* published a poll of the Democratic-controlled Congress, and by a ratio of nearly two to one, the nation's legislators believed the Republican candidate was clearly on the road to victory in the race for the White House. Anderson received little confidence from the poll.

The main reason for Reagan's amazing showing was cited by lawmakers from both parties. Sen. Malcolm Wallop (R-Wyoming) perhaps capsulized it best:

> President Carter's failed economic policies at home and his inconsistent foreign policies will weigh too heavily on voters' decisions for him to win. (*U.S. News and World Report*, September 29, 1980)

Not all lawmakers agreed with his view, however. Rep. Peter Peyser (D-New York) spoke equally clearly from the other side: .

It has become increasingly clear to many people who opposed President Carter that Reagan does not appear to have either a clear grasp of the issues or very good judgment. (*U.S. News and World Report*, September 29, 1980)

It seemed as if Ronald Reagan, from the many public opinion and special interest polls, had a dominant edge on the other two candidates, except for one major factor—escalation toward war.

By September, Jack Anderson (who had correctly tipped Americans on the Cuban missile crisis during Kennedy's Administration—and eight years later was found to be accurate) wrote an article for his syndicated column that was censored by the New York *Times* and several other papers. Anderson released information that indicated that since Carter was lagging behind the Republican candidate, and since it has been proven that even an unpopular president can regain his rallying power during an international crisis, plans were being implemented to mobilize an effort against Iran during October.

Then, as if on cue, neighboring Iran and

Iraq startled the world during the last week of September, bombarding each other's border areas and oil depots. Black clouds billowed over the adjoining enemy lands, causing many to wonder—with good reason—whether an American/Soviet Union confrontation was imminent. As the world tensed, and as each day passed, the Middle East situation grew worse.

Christians especially became concerned, knowing that Afghanistan had been invaded by Russia merely as a link in the Soviet goal to control world supplies of natural resources. The Ribbentrop-Molotov pact, signed in November, 1940, agreed that "the area south of Batum and Baku in the general direction of the Persian Gulf is recognized as the center of the aspirations of the Soviet Union" (*Moody Monthly*, October, 1980). And twenty-five centuries earlier, the prophet Ezekiel had foretold that a great North-South-East Confederacy would march into the Middle East during Israel's latter years (the time when she would once again exist as a nation). Scripture also predicted that Israel (and a few allies—including the "young lions of Tarshish," meaning the descendants of the area now known as Britain) would stand against the military might of Russia, Libya, Ethiopia, Germany, and Turkey—and Persia (now known as Iran). All this is found in Ezekiel 38. With the discovery of oil in the Middle East, this ancient prophecy began to be fulfilled. By early 1980, already a huge military build-up in the Persian Gulf and Mediterranean Sea areas had made the Middle East an armed fortress.

So it was with no small consternation that the United States became increasingly concerned. A war in the Middle East could mean a chain reaction in world events. The question about presidential candidates grew in importance—should the nation trust the incumbent president, who many felt had been reluctant to stand courageously against the Soviet armament build-up? And if not, would they trust a new president who some had labeled as being a Goldwater-like warhawk who might act impulsively? Suddenly, what had seemed to be a lackluster campaign took on life-and-death significance for all Americans.

As news from the Middle East reached a breaking point, Americans watched the all-American performance by the "Gipper" against Carter's last-ditch efforts during the October 28 presidential debate. A straw vote held after the debate by a TV network foretold the inevitable by showing a two to one margin for Reagan.

Yet the media still tried to show the closeness of the race. Some worried that Carter might try a last-minute ploy by "rescuing" the American hostages in Iran, but—for one reason or another—all eleventh-hour efforts seemed ill-fated.

Reagan pollsters, Richard Wirthlin and Robert Teeter, predicted a mild boost because of the debate and late-breaking events in Iran. Patrick Caddell, Carter's polling expert, analyzed a slight Carter edge even up to the final days.

Wirthlin said that the debate erased all doubts about Reagan's character and competence, doubts which the Democratic campaign had worked so hard to develop.

Even the most hopeful estimates of a Reagan lead during the last days before the election were short-sighted, as Americans soon discovered.

By early evening, November 4, 1980, the election results were clear. Despite forecasts of a close popular vote, tallies reported through the evening became, according to ABC's Frank Reynolds, a "Reagan Rampage."

His loss assured by 9:00 P.M., Jimmy Carter congratulated his heir-apparent. Soon after, Anderson, never a viable challenger, followed suit. Both Carter and Anderson had publicly conceded the election to Reagan on national TV by 10:00 P.M.

Ronald Reagan, the euphoric winner, then appeared on TV to tell the nation, "I am not frightened by what lies ahead. Together we're going to do what has to be done. We are going to put America back to work again."

Americans woke up the next morning to shocking final tabulations: "REAGAN'S STUNNING LANDSLIDE SPARKS REPUBLICAN RESURGENCE," screamed newspaper headlines.

By midmorning the day after, theory had become fact. Americans had made a definite statement of belief. The popular vote was 51 percent for Reagan, 41 percent for Carter, 7 percent for Anderson. Electoral votes were even more conclusive; 489 for Reagan to Carter's 49. Reagan carried 44 states to Carter's 7 and Anderson's 0.

One amusing point—even in the midst of a conservative landslide across the nation—was that the media largely ignored the tide-turning voting bloc of evangelical Christians. This was surprising in light of all the ado from the media about "the New Christian Right" during pre-election coverage. Only a few post-election remarks were made by the media concerning the Moral Majority, Jerry Falwell, Pat Robertson, and other evangelicals who played significant roles in the campaign. Interesting!

But even in victory, the new president realized the awesome responsibilities and dangers ahead of him. All through the campaign that began more than a year before, the "zero factor" whispers had become increasingly audible, tersely spoken warnings. Astrology magazines carried the twenty-year-planet-conjunction theme, but with hope that 1980 might begin a new order. Some Christians hoped that since the new president was the eighth in the deadly series, and since eight has often been used in the Bible to signify "new beginnings," perhaps 1980 would indeed mark a change.

The United States Secret Service, however, seemed intent on stepping up security precautions, drawing up the most exclusive danger list in history, containing the names of 400 men and women suffering from an "assassination syndrome" which could drive them to make an attempt on the new president's life. The "deadly 400" (called "demons" by the agents who act as presidential bodyguards) were singled from a larger list of 30,000. According to inside sources, the "demons" were picked because they were all potential killers. Dr. Brian Parker, a Washington sociologist, worked on the studies and reported the findings in an exclusive interview:

This list has been honed down and refined after extensive studies using computers as well as police and intelligence reports.

Many of those on it have made open threats and are on the fringe of insanity. Something inside them has cracked and, for any one of many complex reasons, they are ready to assassinate anyone . . . elected to the White House.

Some of those on the list are after notoriety. Others believe their actions will bring about revolution. Still others have the extraordinary notion that they will be chosen to replace the man they kill.

Some imagine (the President) they are after is specifically working against them. This persecution complex can drive some people to anything.

Secret Service Director H. Stuart Knight,

commenting on the assassination "demons," echoed other bodyguards who candidly (and sometimes off the record) emphasized the incredible task of protecting the president, especially among well-wishing crowds and in the vicinity of Air Force One. Knight said repeatedly to reporters covering the campaign that there would be no way to stop a committed assassin who patiently waits for the right moment, especially when that "demon" does not mind being caught or even dying in the attempt.

"We have the best trained men in the world," Knight said to an unnamed reporter, "but they have a very difficult job. It is *impossible* for us to guarantee safety."

Just as domestic issues and the Middle East had influenced the final tallies in the 1980 presidential results, so the "zero factor" had overshadowed—in one way or another—the entire campaign. Neither the struggles at home nor those abroad would diminish merely because the November 4, 1980, election was finally over. If anything, the battles were just beginning.

So it was with the death cycle. If the warnings had been merely whispered during the campaign, the murmurs would surely increase to headline rumblings. Had the 1980 zero-year president been placed in office by some unseen destiny? Would the coming days in office become a growing, living nightmare as some had predicted? Every tense moment would be another sobering page in *The Presidential Zero-Year Mystery*.

(The President) was seized by a numbing sense of dread. . . how many hundreds—thousands—of others were out there waiting to kill him? How many thousands more lunatics and fanatics were gnashing their teeth at this moment in uncontrollable hatred for *him?* He shuddered. All of these people were unknown to him, never seen, never heard by him, yet all of them were obsessed with *murdering* him. It was a realization as frightening as any nightmare he had suffered as a boy. Yet it was real—and it was irrevocable. Someone was stalking him. Someone would always be stalking him as long as he was President. (*The Zero Factor* by William Oscar Johnson)

10

The Conflict of the Ages

A people may want a free government, but if, from insolence, or carelessness, or cowardice, or want of public spirit, they are unequal to the exertions necessary for preserving it; if they will not fight for it when it is directly attacked; if they can be deluded by the artifices used to cheat them out of it; if by momentary discouragement or temporary panic, or a fit of enthusiasm for an individual they can be induced to lay their liberties at the feet of even a great man, or trust him with powers which enable him to subvert their institutions; in all these cases they are more or less unfit for liberty; and though it may be for their good to have had it even for a short time, they are unlikely long to enjoy it. (John Stuart Mill [Essay on Representative Government])

If the "zero factor" seemed to focus an incredible amount of attention on the 1980 president, no less of a spotlight continued to shine on the country as a whole. Why, in a "Christian" country with an emphasis on civil government, morality, and unequaled liberties, would Americans have to face once again the very real possibility of an assassination or a suspicious death like the seven previous ones? Doesn't it seem a bit unusual—especially since third-world countries that are so prone to revolutions have better averages for longevity of leaders—that America has seen her Chief Executive cut down by bullet or disease every twenty years?

Is it possible that the United States of America has a strange appointment with destiny, and the cost for this fate has been the repeated sacrifice of our zero-year presidents?

Do the answers to the zero-year questions lie somewhere beyond the reach of human hands—perhaps in a supreme being? What kind of gigantic unseen spiritual battle is being waged for America's leaders and people?

The spiritual side of monumental "coincidences" always seems to surface, and the story of God's dealings with America is an exciting saga of modern history that has lasted much longer than the two-hundred-plus years since the official beginning of the United States. In fact, the freedoms (religious and otherwise) seem planned by a guiding hand from centuries ago.

Though archaeological research now records that the Vikings, and possibly the Phoenicians, visited America's shores long before Christopher Columbus did, the Italian navigator has been credited with the discovery of this country. The expedition of Columbus (his first name, Christopher, means "God's messenger"), to the shores of America seems hardly an accident, especially since his personal journals written after three trips to the New World reveal that God spoke clearly to him, reminding Christopher that he had been specifically chosen to be the man to bring the light of Jesus Christ to the New World. Columbus wrote a volume entitled *Book of Prophecies*, and when portions of this book were translated by August Kling (*Presbyterian Layman*, October, 1971), the truth about the adventurer was finally told. Columbus wrote exciting details:

It was the Lord who put into my mind (I could feel His hand upon me) the fact that it would be possible to sail from here to the Indies. All who heard of my project rejected it with laughter, ridiculing me. There is no question that the inspiration was from the Holy Spirit, because He comforted me with rays of marvelous inspiration from the Holy Scriptures. . . .

I am a most unworthy sinner, but I have cried out to the Lord for grace and mercy, and they have covered me completely. I have found the sweetest consolation since I made it my whole purpose to enjoy His marvelous presence. For the execution of the journey to the Indies, I did not make use of intelligence, mathematics or maps. It is simply the fulfillment of what Isaiah had prophesied.

No one should fear to undertake any task in the name of our Saviour, if it is just and if the intention is purely for His holy service.

God had chosen Columbus, a man of prayer and vision, despite his aspirations to find a way to the Far East, to lift the curtain on the New World. The ways of God are not always the ways of man. God could turn the desires of Isabella and Ferdinand for silk, tea, and spices into a new avenue for the gospel (and a one-time-in-eternity opportunity).

Likewise, God's ways were not known to the Pilgrims. The men, women, and children who came over on the *Mayflower* were mainly fleeing persecution in England. Their motivation in emigrating was not primarily to spread the gospel so much as it was to seek freedom in the new land when they arrived on the Plymouth shores on November 11, 1620. They firmly believed God had led them to a new promised land. Under William Bradford's leadership, they composed the "Mayflower Compact," which became a cornerstone for the republic to be established in the new land. A line from the compact verified their covenant with God:

> In the name of God . . . having undertaken, for the glory of God and the advancement of the Christian faith . . . do by these presents solemnly and mutually in the presence of God and one of another, covenant and combine ourselves together into a civil body politic. . . .

This was the first time in history that free and equal men had the opportunity to organize their own God-ordained civil government. The incredible suffering they endured during the seven weeks' journey from England (coupled with the jeering of the *Mayflower* crew) and the terrible hardships of those first winters gave birth to a God-led people in the new land. There are many evidences that only divine providence permitted them to survive (as compared to the "Lost Colony" on North Carolina's shore). A tiny light was flickering on the mere edge of this vast continent, a light that would someday blaze to enlighten the entire world with the gospel of Jesus Christ.

The Puritans had sought reforms in the corrupt Church of England, but persecution had forced them to follow the route of the Pilgrims. John White formed the New England Company and started the exodus of tens of thousands of Puritans from England to the New World. The first Puritans set sail from England in 1629. John Higginson, on board the *Talbot* (one of the five ships), wrote, "We go to practice the positive part of Church reformation, and to propagate the gospel in America." Gov. John Winthrop preached on the flagship's deck, "The Lord will be our God and delight to dwell among us, for we consider that we shall be as a city upon a hill, the eyes of all people are upon us."

Winthrop's words proved to be a prophecy of unusual accuracy. The events surrounding the founding of the United States of America seemed guided by more than mere coincidence. The founding fathers gave allegiance and praise to the Father. The stage had been set for the Revolution by the anointed preaching of Jonathan Edwards and George Whitefield. By the time the Declaration of Independence was written, a feeling of undying freedom and the concept of human equality had been firmly established in the New World.

It is hard for twentieth-century Americans to fathom how radical the phrase, "all men are created equal," seemed in 1776. No government in the history of man had ever asserted, or believed in, the equality of man. And never before had God planted a body of believers in a land that had no existing civil government. Most of the founding fathers confessed that God had guided the new government into being: "We therefore the representatives of the UNITED STATES OF AMERICA . . . with a firm reliance on the Protection of divine Providence. . . ."

It was no unrelated chain of events that allowed the Great Awakening to precede the split with England's tyranny (not to mention King George's taxation attempts). Fervent preaching united the people within the forming nation, and the revivalist influence of deep spiritual perception had penetrated every level of the Colonies. One of the King-appointed governors wrote back to the mother country about the Christian phenomenon:

> If you ask an American, who is his master? He will tell you he has none, nor any governor but Jesus Christ.

And the cry was heard throughout the land—"No King but Jesus Christ."

One of the Revolutionary patriots spoke the mind of the people; even as the outclassed colonialists met the red-coated aggressors, the country felt destiny-led, and Patrick Henry called the people not to forget who was in control:

> An appeal to arms and to the God of Hosts is all that is left us!
>
> They tell me we are weak, but shall we gather strength by irresolution? We are not weak. Three million people, armed in the holy cause of liberty and in such a country, are invincible by any force which our enemy can send against us. We shall not

fight alone. God presides over the destinies of nations, and will raise up friends for us. The battle is not to the strong alone, it is to the vigilant, the active, the brave.

Is life so dear, or peace so sweet, as to be purchased at the price of chains and slavery? Forbid it, almighty God! I know not what course others may take, but as for me, give me liberty or give me death.

And with God in control, what seemed like an impossible war for the weak American colonialists, pitted against the best-trained troops of the world's mightiest empire of the time, became a successful rout. It was no mistake that England needed her forces back for battles on the European continent at crucial times. It was anything but mere fate that allowed the birth of the upstart nation. God had prophesied that the gospel would reach the ends of the earth in the last days, and from the beginning, it was evident that God's hand was on the body of believers whose descendants would someday have the finances and freedoms and methodologies to carry out the Lord's worldwide plan.

That plan seemed nearly defeated before it began. The final peace treaty with England was signed in 1783, and in 1787, the

First Constitutional Convention met. America desperately needed a stable form of government. The convention was a scene of chaos and bitter arguments. Only the dignity and presence of George Washington preserved any semblance of order. It was no accident that two extremely powerful men, the deist Thomas Jefferson and the Quaker Thomas Paine, who might have exerted the wrong influence, were both in Europe at the time of the convention. But even with Washington's sobriety the meetings crumbled into shambles. Finally near the end, Benjamin Franklin, eighty-one years old, himself no great believer in Christ, rose to speak:

> In the beginning of the contest with Britain, when we were sensible of danger, we had daily prayers in this room for Divine protection. Our prayers, Sir, were heard, and they were graciously answered. All of us who were engaged in the struggle must have observed frequent instances of a superintending Providence in our favor. And have we now forgotten this powerful friend? Or do we imagine we no longer need His assistance?
>
> I have lived, Sir, a long time, and the longer I live, the more convincing proofs I

see of this truth: "that God governs in the affairs of men." And if a sparrow cannot fall to the ground without His notice, is it probable that an empire cannot arise without His aid?

We have been assured, Sir, in the Sacred Writings that except the Lord build the house, they labor in vain that build it.

I therefore beg leave to move that, henceforth, prayers imploring the assistance of Heaven and its blessings on our deliberation be held in this assembly every morning before we proceed to business. (quoted from *The Light and the Glory* by Peter Marshall and David Manuel)

Franklin's appeal marked the beginning of a new unity. And in time the more agreeable, God-blessed climate brought forth one of the greatest written miracles, next to the Bible, of all time—the Constitution of the United States of America (England's Prime Minister William Gladstone later remarked that the Constitution was "the most wonderful work ever struck off at a given time by the brain and purpose of man." How little he knew—it was certainly more than man's brain; it is the oldest existing constitution still in use in the world today).

God's hand was also evident in the choice

of America's first Chief Executive. George Washington was offered a kingship, but he refused. In the first presidential elections during 1789, the new nation selected Washington, and the great man wrote his feelings about the awesome responsibility in a book entitled *Daily Sacrifice*:

> Direct my thoughts, words and work, wash away my sins in the immaculate Blood of the Lamb, and purge my heart by Thy Holy Spirit. Daily frame me more and more into the likeness of Thy Son Jesus Christ . . . Thou gavest Thy Son to die for me; and hast given me assurance of salvation, upon my repentance and sincerely endeavoring to conform to His holy precepts and example.

Just as the first president proved to be a man chosen of God for a mighty beginning of the unusual nation, so also the eight years of Washington's presidency were times of an opposing spirit of humanism. Churches, no longer troubled by persecution, became cold. Unitarianism (encouraged by Jefferson) grew rapidly. Men like Thomas Paine attacked the beliefs of the president.

But God was faithful to America, despite the unfaithfulness of many citizens. In the nineteenth century, revivalists like Lyman Beecher, Charles Finney, and Dwight L. Moody were shining stars used by God to bring renewal and awakening to the churches of the growing country.

During the revivals of the nineteenth century, the modern missionary movement was born—clearly one of the greatest reasons for America's free existence. Adoniram Judson is noted as the father of the modern missionary movement; he sparked a new challenge to evangelize the world when he sailed to India (later to Burma). The new concern by Judson and many later missionaries was in startling contrast to European churches, who showed little interest in world evangelization.

By the turn of the twentieth century, revivals began sweeping the nation. Gypsy Smith, Bob Jones, Billy Sunday, and many other well-known evangelists saw thousands, even millions, "walk the sawdust trail." Of those who became Christians, many determined to reach people for Christ around the globe. The Azusa Street revival spawned missionary efforts. Bible colleges were started all over America, and soon Baptists, Presbyterians, Methodists, Pentecostals, and other denominations were training young people to reach the world for Christ. Christian radio programs transmitted the gospel nearly everywhere. Soon literature, records, tapes, and many methods were used as missionary tools. The sixth and seventh decades of the twentieth century opened up opportunities for Christians to be involved in television, and before long, with the advent of satellite programming, the missionary efforts to "reach the world with the gospel of Jesus Christ" became a technological possibility.

God had prepared the nation (and world) for these moments. It was no accident that America had survived war after war, depression after depression, natural disaster after natural disaster. Any thinking American, born again or not, should have been able to see God's hand directly involved with the birth, growth, and protection of the United States. For what reason? Mainly this—95 percent of all financing for world missions and 80 percent of all missionaries come from the United States of America! Why so much from such a small percentage of the world's population? Americans have continued to enjoy an atmosphere of religious freedom in this country. No other nation in the history of mankind has ever seen two hundred continuous years of such religious toleration. Most other nations—even Great Britain and Sweden—prohibit churches from sending funds in any large amount out of the country, but the United States government—based largely upon the Constitution—has allowed a liberality, a tax deduction, and has not restricted sending funds or people to mission fields.

The affluence America has experienced—equaled nowhere in the world—has combined with the liberality of the government in fulfilling Matt. 24:14:

> And this gospel of the kingdom shall be preached in all the world for a witness unto all nations; and then shall the end come.

Obviously God knew He would not be able to depend upon Japan, or Great Britain, or France, or Israel, or Russia, or Germany. He has depended almost totally upon America for the spreading of the gospel. By no small coincidence, America enjoys a most exalted position in the world today. Even with the mistakes, and hypocrisy, and sinister elements—the missionary-minded Christians have been largely responsible for keeping the protection and guidance of God clearly evident in the affairs of the nation.

But the price has been supremely great. Since 1746 (King George's War), America has been involved—with only three exceptions—in blood baths of war *every seventeen years.*

1763   French and Indian War
1776-83   Revolutionary War
1797   Short naval war with France
1812-15   War with Britain
1831-32   Civil War almost began; only President Jackson's firm stand on the nullification issue, and only because South Carolina decided to wait for a more favorable time to secede was the war averted.
1847-48   The Mexican War
1861-65   The Civil War
1881   no war
1898-99   The Spanish-American War
1914-18   World War I
1932-33   no war—war was "outlawed" by the Kellogg-Briand Peace Pact, but the Japanese invasion of Manchuria, and the subsequent avoidance of war opened the door to Hitler and Mussolini—a terrific price to pay for momentary peace—especially since America was pulled into war less than ten years later anyway (1941-1945).

1950-53   The Korean Conflict
1965-68   The Vietnam Fiasco
(Material taken from Gordon Lindsay's
Will Our President Die in Office?)

Further, as God continued to open doors of opportunity for worldwide evangelism during the twentieth century, a tremendous force of corruption and scandal has joined with a small, sinister group to limit the freedoms that have allowed American missionary efforts.

Anytime "conspiracy" is used, "modern" Americans glance away, smirking at the "communist behind every bush" mentality. The truth is, communists—as dangerous and threatening as the "red wave" is—are mere puppets. The Trilateral Commission, mentioned earlier, and its immediate antecedent, the Council on Foreign Relations— are both manipulative puppets of a one-world, "super-rich"-controlled government. Upon close examination, it becomes evident that a select handful of men have been controlling the majority of money and power from all nations—for some time.

In every European war during the nineteenth century, there was always a reshuffling, with a "balance of power" in a new grouping around the House of Rothschild in England, France, or Austria. If any king got out of line, a war would break out in his country, and the "money manipulators" would finance both sides. The war would be decided by which way the financing went. America, of course, became involved during the many wars. The keystone of the international banking empires has always been government bonds, so the international bankers have always encouraged government debt. The higher the debt, the more the interest. Nothing seems to drive governments more deeply into debt than a war. The "select few" always made a "killing" (poor choice of words, perhaps, but fitting) since they usually financed both sides—regardless of the war. For example, during America's Civil War, the North was financed by the Rothschilds' American agent, August Belmont, and the South through the Rothschilds' relatives, the Erlangers.

The same pattern has followed for virtually every war since that time. The 1917 takeover of Russia was paid for by American agents of the international bankers. Communist countries have produced nothing but economic failures, yet "somehow" they have now conquered nearly two-thirds of the world. As mentioned before, communism is not the major threat; economics are much more powerful than weaponry.

And while wars and revolutions have been useful to the "select few" in gaining or increasing control over governments, the key to such control has always been control of money. Under this system, the privately owned monopolies have become an invisible tyranny.

> Those that create and issue the money and credit direct the policies of government and hold in their hands the destiny of the people. (Reginald McKenna, President of the Midlands Bank of England *[None Dare Call It Conspiracy]*)

America had no central bank to control until the country's leaders were "persuaded" through a series of panics, manipulated largely by J.P. Morgan (an American agent for the Rothschilds). "Bank reform" became the cry, and on December 22, 1913, America's Federal Reserve Act was passed in Congress (one of the key bills Woodrow Wilson was told to advocate). The whole central bank concept was engineered by the very group it was supposed to strip of power. How powerful are the men who are appointed by the president to the Federal Reserve Board? The Federal Reserve controls the nation's money supply and interest rates, therefore manipulating the entire economy by creating inflation or deflation, recession or boom, and sending the stock market up or down. Curiously enough, the Federal Reserve Board has never been audited or investigated, since it comes under no regulatory body of the government. In effect, it is a government, unelected and uncontrolled, by itself—proportionally, it is much more effective and powerful than the entire elected government! And here, as in Europe, the men who serve on the Federal Reserve Board are mere figureheads, put in their positions by the "select few" who finance the presidential campaigns of both political parties.

By controlling the economy of a nation, the "insiders" also dictate laws that are most advantageous to themselves.

So while the nations have been fighting each other, spending incredible sums of "borrowed" money, the few "super-rich" individuals who started the wars in the first place somehow manage to look past the thousands of young, dead soldiers, somehow overlook the destruction of nations, and gain even more power. Nobody wins in a war; nobody except the people who financed the killing.

And while Americans have been pointing fingers at "Communists" and "reds" and "pinkos," the invisible manipulators have been laughing.

The most amazing part of the entire worldwide net is this: everybody is a puppet of someone else. People are alarmed at the elected officials who are members of the Rockefeller-owned Trilateral Commission and the Council on Foreign Relations, but even the Rockefellers are puppets of a worldwide select few who "help mold the thinking of national leaders." Some call the few the Bilderbergs, so named for the Hotel de Bilderberg, site of the May, 1954, conference. The group's headquarters is now at Smidswater 1 in The Hague, Holland, a secretive headquarters for the world's most powerful "club." And if this sounds like so much "right-wing" fanatacism, consider the incredible move toward a one-world economy and political system.

But even the top people—among them several Rothschild descendants—are puppets. This is the part that many find hard to believe.

Just as God has guided the direction of the world's affairs and blessed the nations and leaders who have been loyal to Him, so He has warned individuals who are reluctant to follow God's directions (found in His guidebook, the Bible), the "nonbelievers" are "open game" for God's archenemy—Satan. Therefore, the unbeliever allows himself to be manipulated, sometimes by good forces, for a higher evil cause. And that cause is manipulated by another more select group. In the end—Satan is behind *all* manipulations that are evil in nature.

In short—there are two kingdoms, and two separate "networks"—one with God at the head and one with Satan at the head. Unless a person has personally asked Jesus Christ to be his or her Master, he or she *automatically* is Satan's property. Satan also deludes Christ's followers and uses them for his own purposes when he can, just as God often turns evil into good, but the property "contracts" are the final difference.

Two sides—and only two—form the backdrop for the coming gigantic battle between God and Satan (spoken of in Revelation 19 and Ezekiel 38). So far, by comparison, mankind has only seen minor skirmishes.

What part the 1980 presidential campaign and election play in this conflict of the ages remains to be seen. So much responsibility rests upon the shoulders of the man behind the presidential seal. There are so many battles in the spiritual realm over him.

Obviously the question of whether he survives his presidential term or not has become a crucial, critical question. It is much more important than a mere death cycle—there are spiritual issues involved in *The Presidential Zero-Year Mystery*.

11

Can the Death Cycle
Be Broken?

For if the trumpet give an uncertain sound, who shall prepare himself to the battle? (1 Cor. 14:8)

There is a definite death cycle concerning the zero-year presidents—absolutely no one can deny that. The statistics cannot be ignored—that out of all the presidents, most of whom enjoyed relatively long lives, only eight have died in office. Of those eight, seven were zero-year presidents (and the other, Zachary Taylor, died in a zero year).

Since the facts are now obvious, there must be a reason. Some have pointed to a "conspiracy" that has linked together the deaths, but it seems incredible to believe that any group could effectively dispose of America's leaders generation after generation—there are too many human variables involved. Even if some secret-bound group wanted to continue such a dastardly chain of death and chaos that invariably follows an assassination (but why would they do so only every twenty years and, if this group is so powerful, surely they could avoid the election of an unwanted president in the first place), at least some of the deaths—though suspicious in nature—would have to have been caused by some other force.

Now it is obvious that a select few have manipulated history to serve their own needs, and disposed rulers and assassinated leaders have most definitely "served their needs" on occasion, but, as will be shown in this chapter, even the select few are puppets of a higher power.

There are three plausible explanations for *The Presidential Zero-Year Mystery*. America's reaction to the final answer may change the course of history.

The first explanation is *chance.*

It is highly improbable that the "zero factor" is a mere random positioning of possibilities; exclusive statistical studies show that the death cycle should never have existed. The chances against President

Kennedy dying in office were 78 billion 50 million to one. But on November 22, 1963, the incredible odds no longer mattered. If the presidential death cycle remains an incredible coincidence, imagine the nervous excitement among the "deadly 400" and the potentially dangerous 30,000 "demons" that Secret Service Director H. Stuart Knight referred to—many of whom have already made threats and are on the verge of insanity; these men and women—if the cycle is chance-oriented—will be vying for that historic "date with destiny." If the 1980 zero-year president is trapped by fate, even Knight offers little hope, repeatedly warning that there is no way to stop a committed assassin who patiently waits for the right moment and does not mind being caught or even dying in an attempt to change the course of history.

But any thinking person has to realize that *The Presidential Zero-Year Mystery* is no mere chain of coincidences. The twenty-year death cycle since 1840 is a *design that demands a designer.* What happens to the 1980 zero-year president will not be left just to chance. There is a better answer.

Another explanation for the death cycle

is this: some have suggested that *God is the author.*

It is true that God despises a rebellious nation, especially since from the beginning America was a God-ordained, extremely blessed nation. "To whom much is given," Luke the physician once wrote, "much is required." A nation such as the United States, bought and paid for at such a great expense (lives and courage), cannot afford to treat responsibility lightly. God made America great—most of the nation's leaders have agreed on this point through the years—but the struggle to gain power and self-gratification has corrupted all levels of the country.

> Behold, I set before you this day a blessing and a curse; A blessing if ye obey the commandments of the Lord your God, which I command you this day; And a curse if ye will not obey. . . (Deut. 11:26-28)

Is *The Presidential Zero-Year Mystery* a curse from God? This is doubtful. According to John 10:10, God comes to give life, not random death—especially when the death results in chaos for the nation which He has blessed. Plus, there has been no indication to His servants that He would randomly begin a wanton destruction of the zero-year presidents starting with William Henry Harrison; it would seem that God would give a warning to the nation's believers first:

> Surely the Lord God will do nothing, but he revealeth his secret unto his servants the prophets. (Amos 3:7)

If the death cycle is from God, it would seem to be a note of warning with hope, not chaos, for the nation that supports nearly 100 percent of the gospel outreach to the world.

Dr. Billy Graham sees the nation as being at a crossroads:

> First, I believe God is declaring a note of warning to America.
>
> We have been greatly blessed of God in the past—in many, many ways. God has given us a nation with abundant resources, personal freedom and material blessings almost beyond measure. But we have begun to take these things for granted, and use them for selfish purposes. And God is warning us that this cannot last.
>
> More than that, God is warning us about our spiritual neglect and moral indifference. Our nation was founded by men who believed in God, and knew there was right

and wrong in human behavior. But our nation is rapidly losing its spiritual heritage. Secularism, humanism and materialism have engulfed our nation, and if this trend is not reversed we can only expect the judgment of God. The ultimate hope for our nation is not in new political or economic theories. The final hope is a genuine, grass-roots revival in which the hearts of men and women of all backgrounds are turned to God.

Second, I believe God is declaring a note of hope to us today. In spite of the dismal news which blankets our world every day, God is still at work. He is still ready to receive and forgive all who turn to Him by faith in Christ, and He is still ready to give new life and strength to those who seek to live for Him. Everywhere I go in our nation I meet people who have turned to Christ in recent years and are serving Him. Thousands of Bible study and prayer groups have appeared, and these are signs of hope. (Dr. Billy Graham [*Christian Herald* magazine, July/August, 1980])

If the "zero factor" is a warning (or even a curse) from God, there is an answer.

The final explanation for the death cycle is the most grisly of all: can it be that *Satan is the author of the curse*?

Satan *is* the "prince of death." He was a murderer from the beginning (John 8:44). In every instance of murder and destruction, Satan has been close by. And as the presentation of the gospel of Christ has increased, Satanic activity has exploded.

If, in any large city in America, hundreds of deaths were suddenly reported to the authorities, brought about by some invisible gaseous substance, the city would be inundated by a swarming band of newspeople trying to find the causes. The city and national governments would spare no expense to unravel the mysterious deaths. Why then is the country so *blasé* over the "invisible forces" behind the hundreds of deaths, murders, rape victims, cancer-related terminations, and suicides? There has been—in America and around the world—a cover-up of eternal proportions. Relatively few people seem concerned at all over the powerful, invisible forces that continually bombard human beings.

Can there be any doubt that America (and people all over the world) are being used and destroyed by an evil, sinister force? Yet anyone caught pointing a finger at the most powerful conspiracy in the universe—Satan's—is somehow fanatical, unbalanced, uninformed, not-modern, or merely emotional.

If the causes of the plot against mankind, and the secondary conspiracy against the zero-year President of the United States, is to be exposed, the real reasons for it must be identified:

> For we wrestle not against flesh and blood [mere human enemies or conspiracies], but against principalities, against powers, against the rulers of the darkness of this world, against spiritual wickedness in high places. (Eph. 6:12)

Note the last two words—*high places*. The higher the levels of responsibility, the greater the degrees of spiritual warfare.

So, is *The Presidential Zero-Year Mystery* a Satanic curse? Satan has much to gain. America is already in deep trouble. The once-most powerful nation in the world is in a monumental tailspin. Our citizens were defeated and shamed by the Korean Conflict and the Vietnam fiasco. Our international image as world guardian has been shattered, leaving Uncle Sam as a mere figurehead or a "sugar daddy." People have lost confidence in leadership. Economically, America cowers before puny nations who practice oil blackmail. The dollar is losing its value at home and abroad. People are suffering an unbearable load of taxation. Everyone is scared by inflation. Another presidential assassination could signal the chaos that may end up in a declaration of military law and, ultimately, a total change of our entire government (in fact, the Federal Emergency Management Agency, an obscure government agency created by a stroke of Jimmy Carter's presidential pen in June, 1979, stands ready to assume control of the United States government. The FEMA, established by Executive Orders 12147 and 12148, is a shadow government with powers so broad and ill-defined that it could *become* the government whenever the Chief Executive decides to declare a national emergency). Are we on the verge of an Orwellian 1984? A one-world system strong enough to face God's forces has been Satan's acknowledged plan for centuries (see Rev. 17:13). So a presidential assassination might create the "perfect" climate for a takeover of the government that once belonged of, to, and for the people of the United States.

The theory that a curse is the cause of the zero-year deaths is believed among many

American Indians, according to an article in a recent national magazine (*Parade*, September 28, 1980).

During the early 1800s, William Henry Harrison was appointed governor of Indian territory by President John Adams and was charged with protecting Indian rights, but the job also included taking Indian lands to advance the settlement of whites. As the Indians resisted the infraction of their rights, they eventually joined with the British against the Americans. But in the War of 1812, Major General William Henry Harrison defeated the British and the Indian allies who were led by Tecumseh, the great Indian chief. Tecumseh was killed in the Battle of Thames on October 5, 1813.

Supposedly, Tecumseh's brother, Tenskwatawa, "the Prophet," who was a medicine man, confessed a curse upon William Henry Harrison and the United States government.

The curse was that every U.S. president who was elected in a zero year, beginning with Harrison, would die while in office. This legend, known as "the Indians' Revenge," has so far proved true.

A Satanic curse? If so, there is an answer. The 1980 zero-year president need not die while in office.

Whether history's most eerie death cycle can be traced to chance, God, or Satan— the *answer* to *The Presidential Zero-Year Mystery* is found in two verses of history's most complete, workable guidebook—the Bible.

> If my people, which are called by my name, shall humble themselves, and pray, and seek my face, and turn from their wicked ways; then will I hear from heaven, and will forgive their sin, and will heal their land. (2 Chron. 7:14)

Has there ever been a time when healing and forgiveness for America (and the world) was needed more? Some people wonder why God allows such horrible conditions that now exist to continue. The blame is on mankind—not God. God has promised to rid man of corruption and cause peace to settle upon the world, but man ignores the "if" clauses.

Is the future fixed? If so, why did God give "if" clauses? He cannot lie (Titus 1:2, Heb. 6:18). If God makes a promise or covenant, He will not break it. Obviously the gigantic, worldwide Satanic "cover-up" has ignored the real issues and placed the blame on God, rather than on Satan. God's answers work, but only if people act upon His Word.

"If my people . . ." (it doesn't even have to be a majority of Americans—God promised to save Sodom and Gomorrah for only five righteous people).

"Which are called by my name" (the battle lines are already drawn: those identified with Jesus Christ, and all the rest who are—some knowingly, and some in ignorance—being used by Satan).

"Shall humble themselves" (humility is the opposite of *self-gratification* and *personal power*).

"And pray" (prayer is not a collection of mutterings to some superior being, it is a cosmic, physical/spiritual force that is man's link—through the Holy Spirit—to the throne of God).

"And seek my face" ("But if from thence thou shalt seek the Lord thy God, thou shalt find him, if thou seek him with all thy heart and with all thy soul"—Deut. 4:29).

"And turn from their wicked ways" (God would rather manifest mercy than judgment if people would only stop their self-destructive, Satan-glorifying ways).

Then—and only then—will God return the full blessings for America (and the

world). Satan tempts people with good
things, then gives them the evil that was
hidden behind the good. God reveals the
evil first that dwells in mankind's breast,
but offers promises for people to dwell in
peace and goodness. Each person controls
his own destiny, by his obedience or dis-
obedience to God's plan (John 3:16). And
collectively, mankind's acceptance of God's
plan can also make an eternal difference:

> Whenever I announce that a certain nation
> or kingdom is to be taken up and destroyed,
> then if that nation renounces its evil ways,
> I will not destroy it as I had planned.
> And if I announce that I will make a cer-
> tain nation strong and great, but then that
> nation changes its mind and turns to evil
> and refuses to obey me, then I too will
> change my mind and not bless that nation
> as I had said I would. (Jer. 18:7-10, *The
> Living Bible*)

So God can hear from heaven, and forgive sin, and heal the land as those called
by His name meet His requirements—what
does all this have to do with *The Presidential Zero-Year Mystery*? Even during
times of widespread godliness and right-
eousness, zero-year presidents have died
while in office. So even if America does

repent and allow God's intervention, will the 1980 zero-year president still become yet another victim of the death cycle?

The second (and most crucial) part of the answer to *The Presidential Zero-Year Mystery* is in 1 Tim. 2:1-4:

> I exhort therefore, that, first of all, supplications, prayers, intercessions, and giving of thanks, be made for all men;
>
> For kings, and for all that are in authority; that we may lead a quiet and peaceable life in all godliness and honesty.
>
> For this is good and acceptable in the sight of God our Saviour;
>
> Who will have all men to be saved, and to come unto the knowledge of the truth.

Statistics from nationwide polls have proven that only one or two percent of the evangelical Christians in America pray at least once a day for the elected government leaders. Yet God specifically commands His followers to pray for the people in authority, especially for the president (the American equivalent to "kings" in verse two).

God (just as He did in 2 Chron. 7:14) gives requirements—that Christians should pray for their leaders—before He will give the "quiet and peaceable life" (verse two), allow the country to be "good and acceptable" in His sight (verse three), and give the continued freedom for "all men to be saved" (an assurance of world missions in verse four).

Is it any wonder that the American government is controlled by a few unelected, ruthless men? Or is it any wonder that Satan effectively controls the political systems of all countries of the world—including the United States of America? Those are strong words, perhaps, but realistic in the light of the incredible mistakes America has made—and continues to make.

The truth is—if the 1980 zero-year president dies while in office, *God* will not be to blame (He has given a way for mankind to dwell without bloodshed, in peace, but mankind must meet His requirements), nor will some *assassination conspiracy* paid for by the Mob or the "super rich" (they are mere puppets of a higher power), nor even *Satan* (he can be bound and resisted by spiritual Christians—James 4:7; Eph. 4:27; 1 Pet. 5:9), but the real blame will rest squarely on the shoulders of *Christians who refused to pray* for the president and the elected leaders! *God is not going to do what He has commanded His people to do.*

If ever a time has existed when Christians need to intercede for the president—that time is now. There can be no failure this time.

Satan has always placed his forces closely around the leaders of nations. The higher the level of responsibility, the greater the amount of spiritual activity. There are numerous examples, both in ancient times and in the twentieth century.

Israel's first king, Saul, was an infamous example of a God-ordained ruler who became so troubled with the spiritual conflicts buzzing about him that he became paranoid, homicidal, and eventually involved in self-destructive witchcraft; he died a tormented man—knowing he had turned his back upon God.

Saul's successor, King David, began public life as a most God-like young man, used in a mighty way to show God's power, but as the spiritual warfare increased around him, he fell victim to a momentary sexual gratification, and in a tense effort to "cover his tracks," ended by effecting the deaths of his lover's husband, his children, and his children's children. His own nation was cast into a civil war, and the bloodshed that followed created chaos that eventually proved fatal for the nation as it once existed.

As mentioned in Ezekiel 28 (the fallen angels that surrounded the King of Tyre), Satan has attempted to manipulate the thrones of the world through special demonic ambassadors—most of the time he has succeeded. Isaiah 14 also mentions Satan and his special messengers to the leaders of nations.

Daniel, one of the men in the Bible who was faithful in interceding for the leader over him, also wrote about the spiritual warfare centered on kings. In Daniel 10, as he prayed and fasted, Daniel saw a vision of an angel—an angel who had been detained in a twenty-one-day battle with the Satanic "prince" of the kingdom of Persia.

History records similar spiritual battles between the forces of God and Satan over many leaders—in Greece, Rome, Spain, and England. Unfortunately many times Satan's messengers won, and political havoc resulted.

In a not insignificant measure, the American presidents have witnessed a tremendous spiritual battle—the conflicts have already been catalogued for the zero-year presidents.

One of the most noticeable catastrophes

in recent history was the case of Richard M. Nixon. At seventeen, Richard had walked down the aisle to the altar of the Angeles Temple during an invitation given by Evangelist Paul Rader. Dr. Clyde Taylor knelt beside young Nixon as the future world leader prayed the "sinner's prayer." It was a touching, moving conversion. What happened between that time and the shameful resignation during the post-Watergate scandals is not known, but the incredible spiritual conflict that centered on Richard Nixon during the ensuing years was catalogued by the media and the famous tapes. He had godly counsel from men like Billy Graham, but he chose to surround himself with ungodly men. He made the mistake of thinking he could manipulate the "super-rich" manipulators. The price he paid for not making a clearcut decision to give God prominence in his administration was costly.

The language on the early Nixon tapes was respectable and it reflected his well-respected intellect, but as the tapes progressed through the crisis, a degeneration process noticeably deepens, and his vocabulary finally degenerates into a cesspool of vulgarity and obscenities. He was torn between serving God and pleasing the people who owned him. At one point, he made a plea for part of his advisors to pray for him, but the advisors were not prayers. The tragic results that befell the disgraced leader were monumental victories for Satan's fury-filled campaign to weaken the country that had been built upon God's precepts. God doesn't necessarily say that a Christian has to agree with a specific leader, but He still commands the Christian to pray for him or her.

One of the little-publicized successes of Christians praying for a president happened during Gerald Ford's Administration. During 1974, an increasing number of Christians became concerned, feeling perhaps that an attack would be made on the president's life. A growing force of Christians banded together to pray for the president's protection. It was a quiet, powerful exhibition of James 4:7. In a two-month period shortly after the praying began, three brushes with disaster were thwarted.

On September 5, 1975, as the president walked through a crowd of well-wishers in a Sacramento park, Lynette Alice "Squeaky" Fromm, a follower of cult-figure Charles Manson, stood within a few feet of Ford and pointed a .45-caliber semiautomatic pistol at him. After several desperate clicks, the Secret Service agents apprehended Fromm. She began screaming, "It didn't go off! It didn't go off!" Other agents grabbed the weapon and found that the gun was indeed loaded, but for some reason "Squeaky" had not properly loaded the chamber.

On September 22, 1975, Sara Jane Moore pointed a .38-caliber handgun at the president as he emerged from a San Francisco hotel. Oliver Sipple, a retired marine, noticed the gun and hit Moore's hand as the explosion went off. The bullet was deflected, and Ford was not injured.

Less than a month after the San Francisco assassination attempt, the appointed Chief Executive escaped injury during an auto accident near Hartford, Connecticut (October 14, 1975).

In an interview after the second assassination try, Evangelist Billy Graham offered a startling explanation:

> I am convinced that it was angels of God that prevented the assassination of our President and the ensuing chaos that would have followed.

Ford was no less emphatic about the role God had played in the near-tragic chain of events when he said, "It was divine intervention that prevented my assassination."

During the 1976 election bid, Jimmy Carter gave a clear-cut testimony of being a Christian. He used biblical terminology. An increasing number of Christians became aware of the need to support him in intercessory prayer. The results during the next years turned what could have been imminent danger into relative safety.

And now—especially after the 1980 zero-year election, Christians are faced with an incredible challenge to intercede for the president.

Not all Christians are going to agree with the president on every issue. There have been many self-righteous believers who have repeated the well-worn phrase, "Well, if the president is *really* a Christian, how could he possibly do . . . ?" The next time any Christian is tempted to say this, he or she should ask a personal question: "Well, if I am *really* a Christian, how could I possibly do . . . ?"

The truth is that salvation is not based on political platforms, but on a personal faith in Jesus Christ as Savior.

So Christians, though it is healthy to be constructively critical and even unpopularly analytical, do not have the right to refuse prayer for the leader who is over them.

Christians must pray for protection and a "hedge" of God's protective angels to be set up around the president (and the same goes for all authorities).

Christians must pray that the president will seek wise advice, rather than mere puppetry from the "insiders":

> Take away the wicked from before the king, and his throne shall be established in righteousness. (Prov. 25:5)

And Christians must pray that the president will continually follow God's guidance, so that America will always enjoy the freedoms and opportunities we have been given.

There are only two alternatives, clearly presented in Rom. 12:21—"Be not overcome of evil, but overcome evil with good." There is no middle way—not even ignorance, since ignorance breeds neglect, and neglect breeds evil. Christians may use the power God has put at our disposal to overcome Satan's power, or—if we fail to do this—that evil will overcome us. This message from Romans especially applies to Americans, who still enjoy an unequaled freedom to proclaim the gospel to the world.

If Christians do fulfill their function and heed the answers stated in 2 Chron. 7:14 and 1 Tim. 2:14, we will have the power to prevent the coming chaos. But if we do not accept the awesome responsibilities, and if another zero-year president falls victim to the death cycle, and if the course of history is set in a self-destructive direction—Christians will have to face the most bitter eulogy of all—*It Did Not Have to Happen.*

> And I sought for a man among them, that should make up the hedge, and stand in the gap before me for the land, that I should not destroy it; but I found none. (Ezek. 22:30)

God will intervene in most human affairs by invitation only. When a Christian prays for the leaders of the country and says, "Thy will be done, on earth as it is in heaven," he or she is placing in God's hands the legal right to intervene in human affairs. That Christian becomes a channel through which and by which God can move.

Satan worries when the weakest Christians begin to intercede for the president; Satan trembles when two or more Christians join together in behalf of elected authorities:

> Verily I say unto you, Whatsoever ye shall bind on earth shall be bound in heaven: and whatsoever ye shall loose on earth shall be loosed in heaven.
>
> Again I say unto you, That if two of you shall agree on earth as touching any thing [even protection and guidance for the president] that they shall ask, it shall be done for them of my Father which is in heaven.
>
> For where two or three are gathered together in my name, there am I in the midst of them. (Matt. 18:18-20)

But the most workable, powerful verses in Scripture are meaningless and empty unless Christians are willing to practice them. Christians must band together to intercede to break the death cycle and prevent the death of the president, thus preventing resulting chaos and possible loss of religious freedom. That prayer can be similar to this:

> Lord Jesus, we pray for our nation. Send healing to our broken land. We use your Word to rebuke the power of Satan and his

forces. Preserve our president by your grace, and guide all of our leaders in your wisdom. Deliver our nation and the world from further chaos so we may continue to spread your saving gospel.

All the praise we give to you, in the name of the Father, the Son, and the Holy Spirit. Amen.

Will enough Christians band together to intercede for America's leaders? Will the power of the spiritual conspiracy be broken, or will Christians neglect God's commandment to pray? Will the president—like the past seven zero-year Chief Executives—die while in office?

The answers may soon be known. Until then, the puzzle will continue to be shrouded in secrecy—the puzzle known as *The Presidential Zero-Year Mystery*.

Bibliography and Suggested Reading List

Allen, Gary. *None Dare Call It Conspiracy*. Rossmore, California: Concord Press, 1971.

Barzman, Sol. *The First Ladies*. New York: Cowles Book Company, Inc., 1970.

Breeden, Robert L. (chief editor). *The Presidents of the United States of America*. Washington, D.C.: The White House Historical Association, 1978.

Brooks, Stewart M. *Our Murdered Presidents (The Medical Story)*. New York: Frederick Fell, Inc., 1966.

Cleaves, Freeman. *Old Tippecanoe (William Henry Harrison and His Time)*. New York: Charles Scribner's Sons, 1939.

Durant, John and Alice. *Pictorial History of American Presidents*. New York: A.S. Barnes and Company, 1955.

Eaton, Herbert. *Presidential Timber*. New York: David McKay Company, Inc., 1976.

Flammonde, Paris. *The Kennedy Conspiracy*. New York: Meredith Press, 1969.

Ford, Gerald R., and Stiles, Jr. R. *Portrait of the Assassin*. New York: Simon and Schuster, Inc., 1965.

Fuller, Edmund, and Greene, David E. *God in the White House*. New York: Crown Publishers, Inc., 1968.

Griffin, G. Edward. *The Fearful Master*. Boston: Western Islands Publishers, 1964.

Joesten, Joachim. *Oswald: Assassin or Fall Guy?*. New York: Marzani and Munsell, Inc., 1964.

Johnson, William Oscar. *The Zero Factor*. New York: Pocket Books, 1980.

Kelly, Frank K. *The Martyred Presidents (And Their Successors)*. New York: G.P. Putnam's Sons, 1967.

Lindsay, Gordon. *Will Our President Die in Office?*. Dallas: Christ for the Nations, Inc., 1980.

Miller, Hope Ridings. *Scandals in the Highest Office*. New York: Random House, 1973.

Newman, Albert H. *The Assassination of John F. Kennedy (The Reasons Why)*. New York: Clarkson N. Potter, Inc., 1970.

Norton, Howard, and Slosser, Bob. *The Miracle of Jimmy Carter*. Plainfield, N.J.: Logos International, 1976.

O'Toole, George. *The Assassination Tapes*. New York: Penthouse Press, LTD., 1975.

Ray, Jo Anne. *American Assassins*. Minneapolis: Lerner Publications, 1974.

Report of the President's Commission on the Assassination of President John F. Kennedy. Washington, D.C.: Government Printing Office, 1964.

Robertson, Pat. *Perspective* (A Special Report to Members of the 700 Club), 1979.

Russel, Francis. *The Shadow of Blooming Grove*. New York: McGraw-Hill Book Co., 1968.

Senate Internal Security Subcommittee, reports as noted.

Sinclair, Andrew. *The Available Man* (Warren Gamaliel Harding). New York: MacMillan, 1965.

Skousen, W. Cleon. *The Naked Capitalist*. Published as a private edition.

Steinberg, Albert. *The First Ten*. New York: Doubleday and Company, Inc., 1967.

Stormer, John. *None Dare Call It Treason*. Florissant, Missouri: Liberty Bell Press, 1964.

Thompson, Josiah. *Six Seconds in Dallas*. New York: Bernard Geis, 1967.

Wallechinsky, David, and Wallace, Irving. *People's Almanac*. New York: Doubleday, 1975.

Wead, Doug and Bill. *Reagan: In Pursuit of the Presidency—1980*. Plainfield, N.J.: Haven Books, 1980.

Wilson, Vincent, Jr. *The Book of the Presidents*. Brookeville, Maryland: American History Research Associates, 1977.

AUDIO PROPHECY DIGEST

(A David A. Lewis production.)

New one-hour cassette every month.

Sent to subscribers by first-class mail.

Commentary on world events in the light of Bible prophecy.

$30.00 per year

Order from:

David A. Lewis
304 E. Manchester
Springfield, MO 65804